Project Management

FOR

DUMMIES®

PORTABLE EDITION

by Nick Graham and
Stanley E. Portny

A John Wiley and Sons, Ltd, Publication

Project Management For Dummies®, Portable Edition

Published by
John Wiley & Sons, Ltd
The Atrium
Southern Gate
Chichester
West Sussex
PO19 8SQ
England

E-mail (for orders and customer service enquires): cs-books@wiley.co.uk

Visit our Home Page on www.wiley.com

Copyright © 2011 John Wiley & Sons, Ltd, Chichester, West Sussex, England

Published by John Wiley & Sons, Ltd, Chichester, West Sussex

For general information on our other products and services, please contact our Customer Care Department within the U.S. at 877-762-2974, outside the U.S. at 317-572-3993, or fax 317-572-4002.

For technical support, please visit www.wiley.com/techsupport.

Wiley also publishes its books in a variety of electronic formats. Some content that appears in print may not be available in electronic books.

British Library Cataloguing in Publication Data: A catalogue record for this book is available from the British Library

ISBNs: 978-1-119-97441-3 (paperback), 978-1-119-97481-9 (ebk), 978-1-119-97482-6 (ebk), 978-1-119-97483-3 (ebk)

Printed and bound in Great Britain by TJ International, Padstow, Cornwall.

10 9 8 7 6 5 4 3 2 1

WILEY

About the Authors

Nick Graham is the founder and Managing Director of Inspirandum Ltd, a small and specialised company focused on achieving excellence in project management. In his company he has set very clear objectives to teach all project approaches and methods in a practical way so that they can be applied intelligently and productively.

With a career that has covered both the public sector and the private sector, Nick is able to communicate readily with managers in both communities and he's been involved in project consultancy and training for more than 17 years. Nick's experience with structured methods in projects goes back much further where he has specialised in the PRINCE2™ method and is the author of another fine book, *PRINCE2 For Dummies*. More recently he has been involved as joint author of the new, simple-to-use and business-based project management method, PRIME.

Nick is an experienced project practitioner, trainer and author, and he's also a qualified teacher. He runs project management and project risk training events worldwide for companies both large and small, public sector organisations and charities. Those attending his training events have described his style as energetic, lively, fun, very practical and very informative. Nick's consultancy work has ranged from helping to plan individual projects to advising senior managers on how to implement a project method throughout their organisation.

When not away on consultancy or training assignments, Nick lives in Weymouth in Dorset, UK. His wife Kath also works for Inspirandum.

Nick is a member of the Association for Project Management (APM) and the Institute of Directors (IoD).

www.inspirandum.com

Stan Portny, president of Stanley E. Portny and Associates, LLC, is an internationally recognised expert in project management and project leadership. During the past 30 years, he's provided training and consultation to more than 150 public and private organisations in consumer products, insurance, pharmaceuticals, finance, information technology, telecommunications, defence and healthcare. He has developed and conducted training programmes for more than 50,000 management and staff personnel in engineering, sales and marketing, research and development, information systems, manufacturing, operations and support areas.

Stan combines an analyst's eye with an innate sense of order and balance and a deep respect for personal potential. He helps people understand how to control chaotic environments and produce dramatic results while still achieving personal and professional satisfaction. Widely acclaimed for his dynamic presentations and unusual ability to establish a close rapport with seminar participants, Stan specialises in tailoring his training programmes to meet the unique needs of individual organisations. His clients have included ADP, ADT, American International Group, Burlington Northern Railroad, Hewlett Packard, Nabisco, Novartis Pharmaceuticals, Pitney Bowes, UPS, Vanguard Investment Companies and the United States Navy and Air Force.

A Project Management Institute-certified Project Management Professional (PMP), Stan received his bachelor's degree in electrical engineering from the Polytechnic Institute of Brooklyn. He holds a master's degree in electrical engineering and the degree of electrical engineer from the Massachusetts Institute of Technology. Stan has also studied at the Alfred P. Sloan School of Management and the George Washington University National Law Center.

Stan provides on-site training in all aspects of project management, project team building and project leadership. Web site www.StanPortny.com.

Dedication

From Nick: This UK edition of *Project Management for Dummies* is dedicated to Max, one of my grandsons, who with his bright outlook on life, awesome bilingual capability at age 7 and infectious laugh, is an inspiration.

From Stan: To my wife, Donna; my son, Brian; and my son and daughter-in-law, Jonathan and Marci. May we continue to share life's joys together.

Authors' Acknowledgments

From Nick: Writing a book, even when partly based on an existing text, is a long and hard job. I want to thank David Palmer at John Wiley for his vision, support and encouragement which was such a boost to me. Also Simon Bell at John Wiley whose support and input as editor is always so valuable. I have learned to listen very carefully to Simon because though he doesn't say much, when he does he's invariably right.

At home I have, as always, to thank my wife, Kath. Running a small business is usually demanding and Kath takes so much of the pressure to leave me in peace while I work away at the keyboard having fun.

Finally I must thank my friend, Philipp Straehl, from whom I have learned so much in project management, and also those who have attended Inspirandum's project training events. Even when delivering training I am constantly learning more and more about projects as course members share their own insights even while learning material from me. It's very much a two-way street and I am privileged indeed to have worked with so many kind and intelligent people.

From Stan: Writing and publishing this book was a team effort, and I would like to thank the many people who helped to make it possible. First, I want to thank Tracy Boggier, my acquisitions editor, who first contacted me to discuss the possibility of my writing this third edition of my book. Thanks to her for making that phone call, for helping me prepare the proposal, for helping to get the project off to a smooth and timely start, for coordinating the publicity and sales, and for helping to bring all the pieces to a successful conclusion. Thanks to Georgette Beatty, my project editor, and Amanda Langferman, my copy editor, for their guidance, support, and the many hours they spent polishing the text into a smooth, finished product. And thanks to Anita Griner, my technical reviewer, for her many insightful observations and suggestions. Finally, thanks to my family for their continued help and inspiration. Thanks to Donna, who never doubted that this book would become a reality and who shared personal and stylistic comments as she reviewed the text countless times while always making it seem like she found it enjoyable and enlightening. Thanks to Brian, Jonathan, and Marci, whose interest and excitement helped motivate me to see the third edition of this book through to completion.

Publisher's Acknowledgments

We're proud of this book; please send us your comments through our Dummies online registration form located at www.dummies.com/register/.

Some of the people who helped bring this book to market include the following:

Commissioning, Editorial, and Media Development

Project Editor: Simon Bell
(Previous Edition: Georgette Beatty)

Commissioning Editor: David Palmer
(Previous Edition: Tracy Boggier)

Assistant Editor: Ben Kemble

Copy Editor: Charlie Wilson

Technical Editor: Anita Griner

Publisher: David Palmer

Production Manager: Daniel Mersey

Cover Photos: © Imagebroker/Alamy

Cartoons: Ed McLachlan

Composition Services

Project Coordinator: Kristie Rees

Layout and Graphics: Claudia Bell, Carl Byers

Indexer: Potomac Indexing, LLC

Contents at a Glance

Contents

Introduction

*P*rojects have been around since ancient times. Noah building the ark, Leonardo da Vinci painting the *Mona Lisa*, Edward Gibbon writing *The Decline and Fall of the Roman Empire*, Jonas Salk developing the polio vaccine – all projects. And, as you know, these projects were all masterful successes. (Well, the products were a spectacular success, even if schedules and resource budgets were sometimes overrun!)

Why, then, is the topic of project management of such great interest today? The answer is simple: the audience has changed and the stakes are higher.

Historically, projects were large, complex undertakings. The first project to use modern project management techniques – the development of the Polaris weapons system in the early 1950s – was a technical and administrative nightmare. Teams of specialists planned and tracked the myriad of research, development and production activities. They produced mountains of paper to document the intricate work. As a result, people started to view project management as a highly technical discipline with confusing charts and graphs; they saw it as inordinately time consuming, specialist driven and definitely off limits for the common man or woman!

Because of the ever-growing array of huge, complex and technically challenging projects in today's world, people who want to devote their careers to planning and managing them are still vital to the projects' success. Over the past 25–30 years, however, the number of projects in the regular workplace has skyrocketed. Projects of all types and sizes are now *the* way that organisations accomplish work involving development and change.

At the same time, a new breed of Project Manager has emerged. This new breed may not have set career goals to become Project Managers – many among them don't even consider themselves to be Project Managers. But they do know that they must successfully manage projects to move ahead in their careers. Clearly, project management has become a critical management skill for many, not just a career choice for a few.

Even though these Project Managers realise they need special tools, techniques and knowledge to handle their new types of assignments, they may not be able to devote large amounts of time to acquiring them, which is where this book comes in. This book is devoted to that vast majority of Project Managers.

About This Book

This book helps you recognise that the basic tenets of successful project management are simple. The book provides information and explains powerful techniques that help you plan and manage projects successfully. Here, you discover that the real challenge to a successful project is dealing with the multitude of people whom a project may affect or need for support. You find plenty of tips, hints and guidelines for identifying key people and then involving them.

But knowledge alone won't make you a successful Project Manager – you need to apply it. This book's theme is that project management skills and techniques aren't burdensome tasks you perform because some process requires it. Rather, they're a way of thinking, communicating and behaving to help you achieve successful delivery. They're an integral part of how people approach all aspects of their work every day.

We've written the book to be direct and easy to understand. But don't be misled – the simple text still navigates all the critical tools and techniques you'll need to support your project planning, scheduling, budgeting, organising and controlling.

You'll find that we present the information in a logical and modular progression. Examples and illustrations are plentiful – so are the tips and hints. And there's some humour from time to time to keep the writing down to earth. The idea is that you finish this book feeling that good project management is a necessity and that you're determined to practise it!

Conventions Used in This Book

To help you navigate through this book, we use the following conventions:

- *Italics* point out new words and alert you to their definitions, which are always close by. On occasion, italics also add emphasis.
- **Bold** text indicates keywords in bulleted lists or highlights action parts in numbered lists.

We avoid web addresses because they change and the information so quickly goes out of date. However, the text gives enough information for you to search for a particular site or reference.

What You're Not to Read

Of course, we want you to read every single word, but we understand that your life is busy and you may have time to read only what's relevant to your experience. In that case, feel free to skip the sidebars. Although the sidebars offer interesting supplementary information and real-life stories, they're not vital to grasping the concepts.

Foolish Assumptions

When writing this book, we assumed that a widely diverse group of people will read it, including the following:

- Senior managers and junior managers (tomorrow's senior managers)
- Experienced Project Managers and people who've never been on a project team
- People who've had significant project management training and want to catch up on the latest ideas, and people who've had none
- People who've had years of real-world business and government experience, and people who've just started work

We assume that you have a desire to take control of your environment. After reading this book, we hope you wonder (and rightfully so) why all projects aren't well managed – because you'll think these techniques are so logical, straightforward and easy to use. But we also assume you recognise that a big difference exists between *knowing* what to do and *doing* it. You'll have to work hard to overcome pressures that conspire to prevent you from using these tools and techniques. Pressures include any people senior to you who think that if you don't plan and control a project properly, it all works out fine just the same, only you'll have saved time and so deliver faster. Interestingly, the same people don't take that view when organising their family holidays.

Finally, you'll find that you can read this book repeatedly and find out something new each time. Think of this book as a comfortable resource that has more to share as you experience new situations.

How This Book Is Organised

Each chapter is self-contained, so you can read the chapters that interest you the most first, without feeling lost because you haven't read the book from front to back. The book is divided into the following six parts.

Part I: Understanding Projects and What You Want to Achieve

The first part discusses the unique characteristics of projects and the key issues you may encounter in a project-oriented organisation. We look at the life of a project and then focus on its justification – the Business Case – before looking at identifying and managing stakeholders in the project.

Part II: Building the Plans

Part II is fun and practical because it covers the various dimensions of planning, including the very powerful front end to planning, *product led* or *product based* planning. We go on to show you how to develop the project schedule and estimate the resources (both the people and physical resources such as equipment) you need. Then we turn to the essential areas of financial planning and risk management.

Part III: Putting Your Management Team Together

You won't have much success in projects unless you get the people side right. All the plans in the world won't help if your people aren't functioning well. This part covers roles and responsibilities in the project, and then goes on to discuss leadership within the project and how to motivate your team members for success.

Part IV: Steering the Project to Success

Planning is vital, but after the project is running, you must keep it on track. This part explains how to monitor, track, analyse and report on your project's progress and what to do if it goes off track. We also cover the vital area of communications to help you avoid the communications problems that are one of the highest causes of project failure. The part then looks at the end of the project: how to shut down and determine its success before finishing with a quick look at the technology and software you can use to help you. The good news is that if you are short of funds, you can get a lot of really good software (and that really does mean good) for free.

Part V: The Part of Tens

Every *For Dummies* book has this fun part that gives you tidbits of information in an easy-to-chew format. In this part you'll find tips on project planning and writing a convincing Business Case.

Icons Used in This Book

The small icons in the left margins of the book are to alert you to special information in the text. Here's what they mean:

This icon gives a real or hypothetical situation to illustrate a particular point we make in the main text.

We use this icon to point out terms or issues that are a bit more technical, or at least that sound more technical.

 This icon to points out important information you want to keep in mind as you apply the techniques and approaches.

 The Tip icon highlights something you can use to improve your project management practices.

 This icon highlights potential pitfalls and dangers.

Where to Go from Here

You can read this book in many ways, depending on your own project management knowledge and experience and your current needs. However, it's worth starting out by taking a minute to scan the table of contents and thumb through the sections of the book to get a feeling for the topics.

If you're new to project management and are just beginning to form a plan for a project, first read Parts I and II, which explain how to plan outcomes, activities, schedules and resources. If you want to find out how to identify and organise your project's team and other key people, start with Chapter 11 and Part III. If you're ready to begin work or you're already in the midst of your project, you may want to start with Part IV to look for advice on keeping things on track. Or feel free to jump back and forth, hitting the chapters that contain the topics that interest you the most.

No matter how you make your way through this book, plan on reading all the chapters more than once – the more you read a chapter, the more sense its approaches and techniques will make. And who knows? A change in your job responsibilities may create a need for certain techniques you've never used before. Have fun!

Part I
Understanding Projects and What You Want to Achieve

'And now, to tell you about micromanagement,
we have an expert to talk to us.'

In this part . . .

Projects are different from ordinary 'business as usual' work. This first part helps you understand more about the nature of projects, how they are structured and why they are needed. It also helps you answer the question 'Is this really a project?'.

Chapter 1

Project Management: The Key to Achieving Results

· ·

· ·

*R*unning projects well is fast becoming an essential management skill. Many organisations, private and public sector, now recognise that they are losing money and business opportunities unnecessarily because they are failing to plan and control their projects effectively. Companies, charities and public sector organisations are constantly changing, and ever faster, as they adapt to new market conditions, new financial conditions, new business practices, new legal requirements and new technology. Running projects often creates the change, and as a result businesses are increasingly driven to find individuals who can excel in this project-oriented environment.

Taking on a Project

Because you're reading this book, the chances are that you've been asked to manage a project for the first time or that you're already involved in projects and are looking to see whether you can find easier and better ways of doing things. If the project is indeed your first one, that's a challenge and may well give you the chance to excel in something you haven't done before; for many, managing a project even opens a door to a new career. The really good news here, whether you're completely new or have some experience, is that project management has been around for a very long time. In that time, Project Managers have come up with highly effective strategies and a range of very practical techniques. You can benefit from all that experience, and this book takes you through what you need to know.

So, hang on tight – you're going to need an effective set of skills and techniques to steer your projects to successful completion. This chapter gets you off to a great start by showing you what projects and project management really are and by helping you separate projects from non-project assignments. The chapter also offers some insight on why projects succeed or fail and starts to get you into the project management mindset.

Avoiding the Pitfalls

By following a sound approach to the project, you automatically avoid many of the pitfalls that continue to contribute to, or cause, project failure on a mind-boggling scale. You may ask why, if good ways of doing things are out there, people ignore them and then have their projects fail. Good question. People make the same project mistakes repeatedly, and they're largely avoidable. You may have come across the joke by comedian Tommy Cooper:

> *I went to the doctor and said 'Every time I do this, it hurts.'*
> *The doctor said, 'Well, don't do it then.'*

A national public project run in the UK to create a database of offenders for use by the Prison Service, Probation Service and others has attracted heavy criticism for poor management. The National Audit Office, which checks up on government departments, investigated and reported that the project was delayed by three years, and the budget was double the original, but the scope had been radically cut back. Edward Leigh MP, chairman of the powerful Public Accounts Committee in Parliament described the scheme as a 'spectacular failure' and 'a master-class in sloppy project management'.

The following list takes a quick look at the main causes of project failure. The list makes for depressing reading but gives a good background against which to contrast successful project management and the approach in this book.

- **Lack of clear objectives:** Nobody's really sure what the project is about, much less are people agreed on it.

- **Lack of risk management:** Things go wrong that someone could easily have foreseen and then controlled to some degree or even prevented.

- **No senior management 'buy in':** Senior managers were never convinced and so never supported the project, leading to problems such as lack of resource. Neither did those managers exercise normal management supervision as they routinely do in their other areas of responsibility.

- **Poor planning:** Actually, that's being kind, because often the problem is that no planning was done at all. It's not surprising, then, when things run out of control because nobody knows where the project should be at this point anyway.

- **No clear progress milestones:** The lack of milestones means nobody sees when things are off track, and problems go unnoticed for a long time.

- **Understated scope:** The scope and the Project Plan are superficial and understate both what the project needs to deliver and the resource needed to deliver it. The additional work that is necessary then takes the project out of control, causing delay to the original schedule and overspending against the original budget.

- **Poor communications:** Many projects fail because of communication breakdown, which can stem from unclear roles and responsibilities and from poor senior management attitudes, such as not wanting to hear bad news.

- **Unrealistic resource levels:** It just isn't possible to do a project of the required scope with such a small amount of resource – staff, money or both.

- **Unrealistic timescales:** The project just can't deliver by the required time, so it's doomed to failure.

- **No change control:** People add in things bit by bit – scope creep. Then it dawns on everyone that the project's grown so big that it can't be delivered within the fixed budget or by the set deadline.

That's ten reasons for failure, but you can probably think of a few more. The interesting thing about these problems is that avoiding them is, for the most part, actually not that difficult.

Deciding if the Job Is a Project

Before you start to think too deeply about how to set up the project, the first thing to do is check whether it really is one.

You can consider three things to decide if a job is a project:

- Is it a one-off job or something that's ongoing? If the job is ongoing, like taking customer orders, then it's business as usual, not a project.

- Does the job justify project controls? Project management means incurring some overheads but some jobs are so small or straightforward that they just don't justify that degree of control.

- This last one may sound a little weird, and it certainly doesn't fit with the formal definitions; it's the question, 'Do you want to handle the job as a project?' You may choose to deal with a block of work as a project, but I wouldn't – sometimes you have a choice.

Grasping the four control areas

Projects, large or small, involve the following areas of control:

- **Scope:** What the project will deliver
- **Time:** When the project will deliver
- **Quality:** So often forgotten, but an essential dimension
- **Resource:** Necessary amounts of people, funds and other resources such as equipment and accommodation that the project needs

You need to balance these areas for each project, and you can see immediately why so many projects get into difficulties. You look at a project, think about the four control factors and say to yourself, 'They want that scope, to that quality level, with just that resource and by then? They've got to be joking!' Strangely, organisational managers often commit projects to failure by insisting on unachievable deadlines or unrealistic resources. What's even stranger is that those same managers are surprised and even angry when the projects inevitably get into difficulties and fail.

Getting the balance right in the early part of the project when you do the main scoping and planning is, obviously enough, essential. Jerry Madden of NASA, the American space agency, produced a great document called 'One Hundred Rules for NASA Project Managers'. Rule 15 is:

> *The seeds of problems are laid down early. Initial planning is the most vital part of a project. The review of most failed projects or project problems indicate the disasters were well planned to happen from the start.*

It's also useful to think about the four areas of control when dealing with change in the project. Chapter 13 includes a 'four dog' model to help you think about the interdependences. Although many other considerations may affect a project's performance, these four components are the basis of a project's definition for the following reasons:

- The only reason a project exists is to produce the results specified in its scope.

- The project's end date is usually an essential part of defining what constitutes successful performance.

- The quality requirement is a vital part of the balance and may be the most important element. What's the point of delivering an unusable heap of garbage on time and within budget?

- The availability of resources can affect which products the project can produce and the timescale in which it can produce them.

Quality can be a very important factor, and is sometimes the most important, so do think about it carefully. A project to build and install a new air traffic control system for the south of the UK was criticised for being over budget and late on delivery. As a number of people have pointed out, though, if you're sitting in an aeroplane circling while waiting to land at London Heathrow Airport – one of the world's busiest – would you rather that they'd got the air traffic control system in on time and to budget or that they'd got it right?

Recognising project diversity

Projects come in a wide assortment of shapes and sizes. For example, projects can:

✔ **Be large or small:**

- Building a new railway link across London, which will cost around £16 billion and take seven years to complete, is a project, perhaps linked to other projects to form a programme.

- Preparing the annual report for the department, which may take you six days to complete, may also be a project.

✔ **Involve many people or just you:**

- Training all 10,000 of your organisation's sales staff worldwide in the working of a new product is a project.

- Redecorating an office and rearranging the furniture and equipment is also a project.

✔ **Be defined by a legal contract or by an informal agreement:**

- A signed contract between you and a customer that requires you to build a house defines a project.

- An informal agreement by the IT department to install a new software package in a business area defines a project.

✔ **Be business related or personal:**

- Conducting your organisation's five-yearly strategy review is a project.

- Preparing for a family wedding is also a project – and a much more pleasant one than the five-yearly strategy review.

Understanding the four stages

Every project passes through four stages:

✔ **Starting the Project:** This stage involves evaluating the business need for the project, the general approach to performing it, and agreeing to prepare a detailed Project Plan. Outputs from this stage may include approval to proceed to the next stage, documentation of the need for the project, and rough estimates of time and resources to perform it, and an initial list of people who may be interested in, involved with or affected by the project.

✔ **Organising and Preparing:** This stage involves developing a plan that specifies the desired results: the work to do; the time, the cost and other resources required; a plan for how to address key project risks. Outputs from this stage include a Project Plan documenting the intended project results and the time, resources and supporting processes to help create them, along with all the other controls that the project needs, such as for risk management.

✔ **Carrying Out the Work:** This stage involves performing the planned work, monitoring and controlling performance to ensure adherence to the current plan, and doing the more detailed planning of successive phases as the project continues. Outputs from this stage may include project progress reports, financial reports and further detailed plans.

✔ **Closing the Project:** This stage involves assessing the project results, obtaining approvals, assigning project team members to new work, closing financial accounts and conducting a post-project evaluation. Outputs from this stage may include final, accepted and approved project results and recommendations and suggestions for applying lessons learned from this project to similar efforts in the future.

For small projects, this entire life-cycle can take a few days. For larger projects, it can take years! Chapter 2 goes though these stages – the life of your project – in more detail so you can see what you need to be doing and when.

In a perfect world, projects run smoothly and always go exactly to plan. However, because you don't live in a perfect world and because your project certainly won't be running in one, you need to be flexible. When starting to think about your project, you need to allow for:

✔ **The unknown and uncertain:** Projects are rarely 100 per cent predictable. The normal territory of projects is that, to some extent at least, you're going into the unknown. Therefore, your plans need to allow for things going off track. You need contingency; remember Murphy's Law – 'If it can go wrong, it will go wrong.' Chapter 10 has more on contingency and where to place it.

✔ **Learning by doing.** Despite doing your best to assess feasibility and develop good plans at the front end of the project, you may find later on that you can't achieve what you thought you could or in the way you thought you could. When this situation happens, you need to rethink in the light of the new information you've acquired.

✔ **Unexpected change.** Your initial assessments are sound, and your plan is detailed and realistic. However, certain key project team members leave the organisation without warning during the project. Or perhaps the business environment changes and with it your organisation's whole market strategy. Because ignoring these occurrences may seriously jeopardise your project's success, you need to rethink and re-plan in light of these new realities.

The Project Manager's Role

The Project Manager's job is to manage the project on a day-to-day basis to bring it to a successful conclusion. He'll usually be accountable to a senior manager who's the project sponsor, or to a small group of managers who form a project steering committee or project board. The Project Manager's job is challenging. For instance, he often coordinates technically specialised professionals – who may have limited experience working together – to achieve a common goal.

It's important to understand that the Project Manager's position is indeed a role; it's not about status. That's true of all roles in the project and there may, for example, be very senior people working as team members (such as chief engineers and legal advisers) who are accountable to the Project Manager even though in the normal business they're very much his senior. Both team members and the Project Manager himself must understand that he has responsibility and authority in the project that comes with the role, independent of his organisational grade or rank

The Project Manager doesn't do any of the technical work of the project in his role as Project Manager. If he's involved in technical work it's with a different hat on – that of a team member. The distinction is important because if you're doing teamwork as well as project managing, you must be clear about both roles and only wear one hat at a time. It's all too easy to neglect the management and let the project run out of control because you're so engrossed in the detail and challenges of your part of the technical work.

The Project Manager's role requires hard skills such as planning and costing, but also soft people skills, and his success requires a keen ability to identify and resolve sensitive organisational and interpersonal issues. The next section covers the main tasks that a Project Manager handles and notes potential challenges that he may encounter.

Looking at the Project Manager's tasks

Your role as the Project Manager is one of day-to-day responsibility for the project, and that might involve so much work that your job must necessarily be a full-time one. Or it may be that the project is smaller and less complicated and project management is just part of your job. Either way, the responsibilities are the same; it's just the scale and complexity that are different.

- ✔ Sketch out initial ideas for the project, with the justification, outline costs and timescales.

- ✔ Plan the project, including mapping out the controls that will be put in place, defining what quality the project needs and how it will be achieved, analysing risk and planning control actions.

- ✔ Control the flow of work to teams (or perhaps just team members in a smaller project).

- ✔ Motivate and support teams and team members.

- ✔ Liaise with external suppliers.

- ✔ Liaise with Project Managers of interfacing projects.

- ✔ Liaise with programme management staff if the project is one of a group of projects being coordinated as a programme.

- ✔ Ensure that the project deliverables are developed to the right level of quality.

- ✔ Keep track of progress and adjust to correct any minor drifts off the plan.

- ✔ Keep track of spending.

- ✔ Go to others, such as the steering committee, if things go more significantly off track (for example, the whole project is threatened).

- ✔ Report progress, such as to the sponsor or steering committee.

- ✔ Keep track of risks and make sure that control actions are taken.

- ✔ Deal with any problems, involving others as necessary.

- ✔ Decide on changes, getting approval from others where you don't have personal authority to make a decision (for example, when changes involve very high cost).

- ✔ Plan successive delivery stages in more detail.

- ✔ Close the project down in an orderly way when everything's done.

So, the tasks will keep you very busy but they will also be very enjoyable if you're a Project Manager at heart.

A key to project success is being proactive. Get out in front of the project and direct where it's going. Don't follow on behind the project being reactive and having to fire-fight countless problems because you didn't see them coming.

Avoiding 'shortcuts'

The short-term pressures of your job, particularly if you're fitting in project management alongside other work, may tempt you to cut corners and leave things out. That's not the same as adjusting the project management needs to the project, but rather missing stuff out altogether that you really should have done. Resist the temptation to cut corners, because usually doing so comes back and bites you later when you face unnecessary problems, and delay, in the project.

Chapter 2

Thinking Through the Life of Your Project

In This Chapter

▶ Understanding the lifespan of the project

▶ Seeing the different characteristics of each stage

▶ Knowing what to do at each point in your project

▶ Dealing with project documentation and not letting it take over

*T*his chapter covers the lifespan of the project from the initial idea through to closure. Sometimes seeing how things like business justification, planning and risk management fit into a project can be difficult until you have the big picture, so this chapter provides that big picture. It explains what you need to do and when, and also covers two key project documents.

Being Methodical

Projects have a sequence from the first idea through to closure, and this chapter provides you with a simple, clear structure. If you want to move on to a more detailed approach, you can use a structured project methodology such as:

✔ **PRINCE2 (PRojects IN a Controlled Environment):** Owned by the UK Government

✔ **PRIME (PRoject Implementation MEthod):** A powerful but straightforward business-focused project method that Nick Graham, co-author of this book, has helped produce

Other methodologies include those associated with tools like Microsoft Project and those developed by major consultancies for use with their clients. In all cases, methodologies offer a structure that takes you through your project. PRINCE2 is rather more complicated than most because it has processes that don't run in a straight sequence. (Find out more in Nick's book *PRINCE2 For Dummies*, published by Wiley.) In contrast, this book sets out the work of project planning and management in a simple and linear way.

Breaking the Project into Stages

Just about all project management approaches break projects into stages, or you may know them as *phases*. Chapter 1 set out the four main stages in any project:

- ✔ Starting the Project
- ✔ Organising and Preparing – the project planning
- ✔ Carrying Out the Work
- ✔ Closing the Project

Of these stages, the third one – Carrying Out the Work – can repeat, so you can have more than one delivery stage. In a small project, you may decide on a single delivery stage, but in most projects you have several. You can see a project example with two delivery stages in Figure 2-1.

Figure 2-1: The stages of a project, with two delivery stages.

The unofficial stages of a project

Some unofficial stages – author unknown!

✔ Enthusiasm

✔ Disillusionment

✔ Panic

✔ Search for the guilty

✔ Punishment of the innocent

✔ Praise and honour for the non-participants

Some say that the first stage, Starting the Project, isn't part of the project but is rather preparation beforehand to include things such as checking to make sure that the project really is a project. That's a logical argument, and Figure 2-1 reflects it.

If you go with the idea of Starting the Project not actually being part of the project, then the project starts for real with the full planning in the second stage.

Seeing the advantages of stages

Breaking the project into stages has many advantages. Take these four, for example:

✔ Stages allow everyone to concentrate on one part of the work at a time.

✔ They break up the detailed planning into convenient blocks, and you plan each delivery stage in detail just before that stage starts and using the latest information.

✔ It allows the sponsor or steering committee to stay in firm control of resource by authorising one stage at a time.

✔ It provides a clear point when each stage ends, usually called a *stage gate*, for checking that the project is still in control and remains viable.

Deciding on the number of delivery stages

How many delivery stages should you have? Well, it all depends.

The first thing to say about delivery stages is that they're not all the same length. They're not timed units of, say, one month long. Rather, delivery stages reflect two main criteria:

- Blocks of work that are cohesive and where things belong together

- Amounts of work that the sponsor or steering committee is willing to authorise at a time – the amount may vary at different points in the project according to, for example, the degree of risk in that part of the project

The end of each stage is marked by a stage gate meeting with the sponsor or steering committee. The gate is a useful control point to take stock and check that the project is on track.

A few stage decision factors

Some factors to bear in mind when deciding on stages:

- Sensible, cohesive blocks of work

- Staying within a maximum spend; for example no stage is to be more than £1 million. You may also need a stage gate just before that major investment in equipment to be sure the project is still okay

- Staying within a maximum time decided by the sponsor or steering committee; for example no stage is to be longer than two months

- Important business events; for example financial year end or the publication of a major strategy review for the company that may trigger a substantial change to the project

- How business critical the project is and the degree of risk involved

- Who the Project Manager is: if the Project Manager is very experienced, then the sponsor may be happy with quite long stages and few of them, but if the Project Manager is inexperienced, then you need shorter stages and more of them

Understanding the Main Stages

The rest of this chapter focuses on each of the stages in turn, looking at what you need to do at each stage and the main project management documents you deal with.

Starting the project

Three reasons for having the Starting the Project stage are:

- ✓ **You need to know whether the project is worth doing.** Unfortunately not all ideas are good ideas. Rather than rushing into full planning, having a quick look at the idea makes sense before committing more time and resource to it.

- ✓ **You need to get basic information together.** You won't find it easy to plan the project if you haven't established, at least in outline, what the project is, what resource is available and any constraints such as on the delivery date.

- ✓ **You're best sketching out the idea for the project and getting agreement before going on to full planning.** If you leap straight in to full planning to save time, you often discover that disagreement arises when people check the plans, because they have different ideas about the project even though they're using the same words.

Understanding the characteristics

The main thing to remember about Starting the Project is that you need to go fast. A common mistake is confusing Starting the Project with the next stage of Organising and Preparing, which takes a while. It's likely that Starting the Project will take a couple of days and it may just be a couple of hours, even for a fairly substantial project.

Imagine that you're a rich and successful Project Manager (or perhaps you don't have to imagine it) and you want a huge house built for you. You go to an architect and say, 'I'd like you to build a house for me please.' What does the architect reply – 'That's fine, I'll come back to you in eight weeks with some scaled drawings'? No, the architect says, 'That's fine. Please take a seat and let's talk about what you have in mind, and we'll do a sketch plan.' The architect starts with a sketch, not a beautifully finished scale drawing. So it is with Starting the Project. You do a sketch 'on the back of an envelope' to check whether the project idea is a good one and whether it's worth going on to full planning.

Knowing what to do

In Starting the Project, you think roughly what the project is and whether it's worth continuing to the next stage to do the full planning. You look at six key areas:

- ✔ **Objective:** What exactly is the objective of the project? To save money perhaps, or speed up the ordering procedures? You need to make sure everyone's clear on the objective(s), has thought it through and agreed it.

- ✔ **Scope:** What's the project intended to cover and, usefully, what won't it cover if some areas are unclear? What will the project finally deliver?

- ✔ **Resource:** How much do you expect the project to cost? Be realistic here. How much staff resource will the project need, and will it need particular skills? The resource figures are very much ballpark ones at the moment because the planning has yet to be done.

- ✔ **Time:** How long is the project likely to take, on the assumption that resource can be provided when it's needed? Again, this is a ballpark estimate.

- ✔ **Justification:** Why do you want to run the project? Perhaps this is a no-brainer because the project is mandatory – head office has instructed that each regional office runs a project to review its local client base. Normally, though, the project is justified because of benefits such as greater market penetration, lower costs or faster customer service.

- ✔ **Constraints:** Will anything influence the way that the project is run, or even what it delivers and when? For example, it might be time critical. You should also think about the required quality level of the project, such as whether it's 'quick and dirty', safety critical or, usually, somewhere in between.

Thinking about management documents

Unless you have a very small project for which you can keep the full detail in your head, and nobody else needs to read anything about it, you're going to have to write some things down. The trick here is to keep documents to the minimum and to 'think wide' about how you communicate information. You can find more on documents in 'Organising and Preparing', later in the chapter.

Projects seem to attract paper (and the electronic equivalent) like doctors' surgeries. The PRIME method has a catchphrase in its business-focused approach that's worth repeating here: 'If there's little to say, say little.' Keep your project documentation trimmed down or you'll drive up project costs and push out the delivery date.

For the Starting the Project stage you need to write down the information you find out in the form of an outline document that others, such as steering committee members, can read and then approve or reject. However, don't get too detailed. Although the information is in a document, you may well discuss the content in a meeting or give a short presentation to the decision makers and give out the document as a backup.

Organising and preparing

Ah, so the members of the steering committee loved the idea, did they? Well done on your presentation of the Project Outline. Okay, on with the next stage then: roll your sleeves up and get down to the real work of project planning.

Understanding the characteristics

The Organising and Preparing stage gets you ready for the delivery stages of the project. It covers the overall planning of the project, and also the detailed planning of the first delivery stage. If the sponsor or steering committee says 'go' at the end of the Organising and Preparing stage, the first delivery stage can start immediately, because the detailed plan for it is already in place.

When thinking through this stage, balance the work very carefully. A major cause of project failure is poor plans or a complete lack of plans. The answer to that problem isn't to go to the other extreme of developing excessively detailed plans for everything. Over-planning just wastes time now, and then again as the plans are maintained throughout the project. Because things will almost certainly have changed since the start of the project that maintenance will include re-working the detail, making much of the initial work a waste of time.

The Body family

This is a story about four people named Everybody, Somebody, Anybody and Nobody. There was an important job to be done and Everybody was sure that Somebody would do it. Anybody could have done it, but Nobody did. Somebody got angry about that, because it was Everybody's job. Everybody thought Anybody could do it, but Nobody realised that Everybody wouldn't do it. It ended up that Everybody blamed Somebody when Nobody did what Anybody could have done.

Author unknown

The approach of developing a high-level Project Plan now and then more detailed stage plans as you approach each delivery stage, gives you good control. As with most work, use the KISS principle for planning: **K**eep **I**t **S**imple, **S**tupid! Start simple and only get complicated where really necessary in order to exercise sufficient control over the project.

Knowing what to do

For the detailed planning work, you need to investigate a number of areas, and usually that means consulting other people. You may be a subject expert and need little advice, but Project Managers don't necessarily have to be subject experts and so often need to get input from people who are.

Some of the areas will be developed into more detail from the high level information set down in the Project Outline.

✔ **Scope:** Now it's time to finalise the scope. Say exactly what the project will cover and deliver and also, if you identify areas that could otherwise be misunderstood, what it won't cover. Chapter 3 has more on this.

✔ **Business Case:** The Business Case sets out the full justification of the project, including its costs, and also defines the business benefits that the project will deliver and the way in which those benefits will be measured. See Chapter 3 for much more on the Business Case.

✔ **Project Plan:** The Project Plan is a high-level plan of the delivery stages and closure stage, although the closure stage may be particularly tentative at the moment. The Project Plan sets down what the project will deliver, the activities, and the staff resource and finance involved. Part II of this book gives lots of practical advice on planning and some really powerful techniques to help.

✔ **Risk:** You should look at the risk involved in the project and also the means of controlling it. Chapter 9 helps here with some useful techniques. Some people question whether you really need risk management in every project, even the very small ones. Yes, you do.

✔ **Quality:** In the Project Outline you've already indicated the quality level needed for this project. Now is the time to establish exactly how you'll carry the quality through into the deliverables, what degree of control you need to exercise, and how you'll audit to make sure that the required quality has been delivered. Chapter 5 has more.

✔ **Roles and responsibilities:** Who needs to do what in the project? You probably decided this back in the first stage, but it's worth setting down roles and responsibilities now, with any adjustments. In that way, everyone involved knows what they should be doing on the project and, importantly, what everyone else should be doing as well. That helps avoid communications problems where things fall down the gaps. You can read much more on roles and project organisation in Chapter 10.

✔ **Communications:** You need to think through the communications carefully, because this area is a major cause of project failure. Chapter 14 goes into full detail.

✔ **Controls:** For a very small project don't get carried away, because you probably won't need many controls at all. In a larger project, though, you need to think through controls carefully.

Thinking about management documents

You should document all planning and control areas, albeit simply on small projects. On larger projects, expect the documentation to be more substantial. Remember the balance of having sufficient information to define and control the project but not more than that.

The name given to the main planning document in the Organising and Preparing Stage is often *Project Charter*, but other terms are in use that you might recognise, such as Project Plans, Project Definition Document (PDD) or Project Initiation Documentation (PID).

Control areas to consider

Some areas to bear in mind when considering controls include:

✔ **Project Manager authorities,** such as spending limits and decision-making limits on things like change and adjustment of the project

✔ **Reporting,** covering the frequency and content of reports

such as those for progress, finance and risk

✔ **Flexibility,** including whether the Project Manager can proceed with a certain amount of a following stage (percentage, value or time) if a short delay occurs in getting the steering committee together for a stage gate

---

The Project Charter is used to define the project and say how it will be controlled. The charter also will form a information base for a decision on whether to run the project, then as an ongoing reference for those coming into the project later on.

Along with the charter, you also need the stage plan for the first delivery stage, so you can proceed without undue delay.

Carrying out the work – delivery stages

This is the stage that usually repeats; you can have multiple delivery stages.

Understanding the characteristics

This stage is simple in concept, as its title suggests. The delivery stage(s) is where the teams build project products and test them, so it's the main part of the project.

Knowing what to do

In a delivery stage, you give work out to teams, get progress information back in, and keep track of where the stage is. If the stage is going off the plan, you need to establish why that is and take action to get it back on track. That adjustment is part of the routine 'steering' that you need to do throughout.

If things go off track by more than an amount set by the sponsor or steering committee, then you need to refer the matter back for discussion and a decision.

You also need to make allowances for unplanned stuff. You must allow time, and perhaps the time of other people, to deal with things such as problem resolution and changes.

Towards the end of each delivery stage, you'll need to do the more detailed planning for the following stage and update the Project Charter as necessary.

Thinking about management documents

During the stages, you produce regular progress information for the sponsor or steering committee, and towards the end of each stage, you also produce a stage plan for the next stage.

Progress

It's important for a number of people, both inside and outside the project, to be kept up to date on the project's progress. The Communications Management Plan can include quite a list of people who need to get a copy of progress reports such as organisational managers and managers of other projects.

Stage Report

Depending on what the sponsor or steering committee wanted and on how formal the project is, you may need to produce a report at the end of the stage to record how it went and what the final figures are on cost and time.

Closing the project

Normally you have work to do to close down the project and release resource, and on the technical side to deal with any teething problems and adjustments. This section is a summary and you will find much more on closure in Chapter 15.

Understanding the characteristics

In the Project Plan, prepared at the start of the project, the closure work is uncertain and so the plan is tentative. As you approach the end of the final delivery stage, everything is clear and you can plan closure with confidence.

A Project Charter

Some of the areas in the Project Charter develop those you sketched out in the Project Outline, and others are new. In all cases, though, adjust the content of the Charter to meet the needs of the project. Excessively big charters aren't impressive; they just make work for everyone. Inadequate charters don't define the project or its controls sufficiently well to run the project.

- **Objectives:** The agreed objectives for the project.

- **Scope:** What's included in the project, and what's excluded where confusion may exist.

- **Business Case:** The justification of why the project is being run, together with a list of benefits and how benefits will be measured.

- **Roles and responsibilities:** Who's doing what in this project? This section can also list the stakeholders – those with an interest in the project.

- **Communications Management Plan:** What information will be moving about and how it will be communicated, including reports

within the project (which may be verbal).

- **Quality Plan:** The level of quality that's needed, how the project will achieve the quality, and how the project will be audited to be sure that the quality has indeed been achieved.

- **Risk Plan:** How risk will be controlled in the project and who's responsible for it.

- **Project Plan:** Information on what will be produced, the activities needed, and the required resource, notably in terms of finance and staff time.

- **Control procedures:** In anything other than a small project, people need a clear statement of procedures such as for problem reporting. This section also can set down the Project Manager's authority limits and the procedures for referring anything beyond the Project Manager.

- **Constraints:** Anything that affects how the project is run and delivered, such as security, a fixed delivery date for the project, or limitation on the type of equipment used.

Knowing what to do

In closure, you need to evaluate the work required to sort out any teething problems and then wind down the work and hand over to operational support. You may have already agreed some of the handover, and it may be subject to legal arrangements such as when handing over a new building.

On the project management side, you need to produce documentation needed now and for the future (such as for maintenance) and store it. Finally, you produce a Project Report to give final costs and the level of any business benefits that you can already see and measure at the end of the project.

Thinking about documentation

You need to break the documentation down into two groups: information to be kept about the project itself, and information to be sent to others for action:

- ✔ **Project information:** A Project Report and operational documentation such as that needed for maintenance.

- ✔ **Outbound information:** Ongoing work, such as risk management needs, as well as information such as lessons learned in this project which may benefit future ones.

Chapter 3

Defining the Project and Producing a Business Case

· ·

In This Chapter

▶ Setting down clearly what your project will cover, but also what it won't

▶ Writing a Business Case – the justification for the project

▶ Understanding the different types of benefit

▶ Avoiding the pitfalls of Business Cases

· ·

*A*ll projects are created for a reason – you identify a need and devise a project to address that need. You then determine the success or failure of the project by how well it meets that need and whether it delivers the business benefit that justified expending all the effort on the project in the first place. This chapter helps you develop clear boundaries for the project – the *scope* – and then set down the justification, or *Business Case*, for running the project.

The scope and Business Case go hand in hand. Each affects the other, so thinking about them together is helpful. The Business Case lists the business benefits of running the project; it may be worth adjusting the scope in order to get better business benefits. Equally, it may be advantageous to chop another part of the project out because it isn't absolutely necessary and very few benefits exist in that part to offset the work involved – it just isn't worth it. The scope, then, is the 'What?' and the Business Case is the justification, the 'Why?'

Although you may need to adjust the degree of formality from project to project, you shouldn't ever leave out the work of defining the scope and justifying the work. You always need to be clear about what you are covering in the project, and you should always be very clear about why you want to do that work – well, unless you're intent on wasting your effort and that of other people and then delivering the wrong thing as a crowning glory.

For the Business Case in particular, you sometimes need to be more formal than at other times. But you always need to write things down in an ordered way if someone other than you has to approve the project. You may have to work to a set format if you'll have to go through some organisational approval process such as getting the go-ahead from a finance committee. This chapter shows you what's involved, helps you think about the Business Case clearly, outlines a few techniques, and even helps you side-step some Business Case bear traps.

Defining the Scope

The *Scope Statement* is a written statement that sets down exactly what the project will cover, and usually also what it won't. Both the people who requested the project and those managing it (including the sponsor or steering committee) should agree to the Scope Statement before any work begins in the delivery stage(s).

Although, obviously, stating clearly what the project will cover is important, additionally setting down what it won't (*negative scope*) is often really helpful. The negative scope isn't the whole world outside the intended project, but rather things that people involved in the project could confuse.

Managing expectations

Misunderstanding the scope when agreeing it is so very easy, and this isn't necessarily because the Scope Statement is imprecise or careless. Rather, misunderstanding comes from the age-old problem of people seeing what they expect to see, even if it isn't there, and making unconscious assumptions. Even worse is when busy managers sign off the Scope Statement having only skim-read the headings while grabbing some water from the cooler between meetings. What's that? Oh no, not in your organisation, of course. Your managers are always very thorough and read important documents with great care, but in *other* companies . . .!

At the end of the project, a common problem is that people look at the deliverable, such as a new computer system for accounting, and a conversation develops with the development team along these lines . . .

'I can't see the invoicing function on the main menu.'

'Err. The system doesn't do invoicing. We never set out to include invoicing.'

'What? You can't have an accounts system without invoicing!'

'Well, actually you can. This is one.'

'But we need invoicing.'

'Look, here's the Scope Statement from the Project Charter listing all the functions we were going to include, and here's your signature on the bottom where you signed the statement off to agree it, and it doesn't mention invoicing . . . does it?'

'Oh no, you're right. It doesn't . . . but we need invoicing!'

How simple would it have been to say in the Scope Statement right at the beginning of the Starting the Project stage (see Chapter 2 for more on stages), that the planned system will include this, this and this, but exclude that, that and invoicing? Defining the scope properly is about managing expectations. People are clear about what they'll be getting when the project is delivered, but are also clear on what they won't be getting.

Challenging the scope

The negative scope could well lead to a challenge. Continuing with the invoicing example from the last section, if the scope says that the new accounts system won't include invoicing, this may then be challenged by those asking for the system, who say that actually they need it included. Indeed, if time and funds are limited, they say, they'd rather have invoicing than a couple of the other functions listed. That leads to a change of scope, and the project will be all the better for it.

You're better off discussing and changing the scope when developing the Project Charter (see Chapter 2 for more on this document) than in the depths of the project when it slowly starts to dawn on those receiving the project deliverables that they aren't getting quite what they wanted. Better still, however, is discussing the scope when producing a Project Outline in the Starting the Project stage. When you discuss and adjust the project boundary while the plan is still a sketch, making changes requires relatively little work. Clearly, though, making changes after you're into more detailed planning is a much bigger job.

Grasping the extent of scope

A dictionary definition of scope is 'the extent of the area or subject matter that something deals with'. In your case, the 'something' is the project. So what's the extent of your project? You can define the scope in one or more of the following ways:

- **Deliverables, or products:** In many projects, setting down scope in terms of what the project will deliver is helpful. Yes, the end product, but also any significant products along the way.

- **Functions:** This is useful for new or revised systems (whether they're computer ones or procedural ones). Which functions will the project cover and which won't it cover?

- **Geography:** Which areas of the organisation will the project cover, for example just your offices in Scotland or just three departments at your corporate headquarters?

- **Time:** A more unusual scope definition, but valid and helpful for some projects. The project will cover all work on this subject area between now, when nothing's been done, up to the end of the financial year, when the project must deliver a management review document.

Being clear

When thinking through the dimensions of scope and writing it all down, think about who'll be reading the Scope Statement in order to approve it. It's no good filling the Scope Statement with all sorts of technical detail if it must be agreed by people in the business area who don't understand such things. The scope must communicate, and must do so particularly to the sponsor or steering committee: they must be able to sign off the Scope Statement to say, 'Yes, that's the project we want, and that's what we're willing to pay for.' On the other hand, the Scope Statement must be specific, so don't shy away from detail where you need to spell things out. If that does include some technical stuff, then put in a plain-language explanation.

Put simply, if you're asking people to sign off a Scope Statement, make sure it's one they can understand and so confirm. It's in nobody's best interests, including yours, for sponsors to sign off documents that they don't understand and are having to take on trust.

Prioritising

When you first think about the scope of the project and talk about it with others, you often find that not everything is essential. In your new car project, wheels are pretty impor-tant, but lights on the mirrors on the sun visors, while nice, probably aren't essential. It can be a real help, then, to priori-tise the requirements.

Some use the MoSCoW approach to help with prioritising:

- ✔ **Must have:** The essentials; the project must address all these elements.

- ✔ **Should have:** High priority, but not absolutely essential.

- ✔ **Could have**: Useful and worthwhile, but lower priority.

- ✔ **Won't have:** Something suggested but now not consid-ered worthwhile, or that will be held over, perhaps for a later enhancement project.

Producing a Business Case

Having got the scope clear, although you may go back and adjust it, it's time to look at the justification for the project – why your organisation should do the project. This is the Business Case.

Getting to grips with the basics

You can adjust the contents of the Business Case to suit the project and also any organisational standard or methodology you're using. Here are the basic contents that you'll need as a minimum for any project:

- **Benefits:** Information on the benefits, but usually also when they'll come on stream, when they'll be measured, buy whom and how.

- **Context:** For example, the fit with the organisational five-year strategy or just to say it's a small stand-alone project to improve performance in a particular area of the business.

- **Cost:** Ballpark at first, but kept up to date as better information comes to hand.

- **Justification:** Is the project solely benefits driven, or does it have any element of compliance, such as there being a legal requirement to run the project?

- **Timescale:** A rough estimate at first, but updated from better information later.

Updating the Business Case

The Business Case is one of the most important documents you'll have in your project. It shows the justification for doing the project in the first place, but it's then important when monitoring ongoing viability. If, for example, part way through the project, circumstances change and the benefits projections now fall through the floor, you probably want to shut the project down. It follows that you're going to have to keep the Business Case up to date throughout the project if it's to remain helpful in monitoring the viability of the project and as an aid to decision-making.

Keep a copy of the Business Case when it's approved at the start of the project and again at every approval point such as a stage gate (the end of a stage; see Chapter 2 for more). But keep the Business Case up to date and so immediately usable to help check the impact of changes to the project and changes in the environment in which the project is running.

Justifying the project

When you take on a project you may need to go and talk to a few people and look in a few places to help you get the justification clear. For example, find out who had the original idea that led to your project and talk to them. Also go and talk to the end users of the project deliverables as they can normally help assess the benefits. Then you may also find information in documents such as:

- ✔ Correspondence and emails referring to the project
- ✔ Minutes from division, department and organisation-wide planning and budget sessions
- ✔ Reports of planning or feasibility studies

Although they may not have initiated the idea, other people may benefit from your completed project. They may also be able to contribute information to help with the Business Case. Think about people including business partners, clients, suppliers and operational staff.

Identify these other people as soon as possible to determine what their particular needs and interests are and how you may need to address them.

As you identify and note down people who can benefit from your project, you can also note down those who'll oppose it. This helps with your stakeholder analysis which you will find more about in Chapter 4.

Understanding the justification

There's a tendency for senior managers to think that all projects must have business benefits to be viable. That's not right thinking, though, and other perfectly valid reasons exist for justifying projects. Having said that, business benefit is the most common justification. Justifications may include:

- ✔ **Business benefits:** Things such as cost savings, better customer service, improved profits, better market penetration.

✓ **Compliance:** Relates to projects that are compulsory, even if they bring no business benefits. This includes legal and organisational compliance.

✓ **Enabling:** The project doesn't provide any business benefit in the normal sense, but does something that allows other projects to run, and those projects will deliver business benefit.

You can, and often do, have a hybrid Business Case that has more than one type of justification. For example, your organisation may have to run a project for legal compliance, but the project will nevertheless deliver some business benefits. Although those benefits won't completely pay for the project, they'll at least offset some of the costs.

Understanding benefits

Within the justification, it's important to appreciate the differences between three types of benefits:

✓ **Direct saving:** A direct saving is where the organisation will save real money. If you change an old machine for a new one, the maintenance costs of the new one will be substantially less. The saved money will be in the maintenance budget, and it's real; you're going to get that cash saving.

✓ **Quantifiable benefit:** This is a saving that you can measure in money terms, so it's *quantifiable*. However, you probably won't see the actual money. For example, a new procedure that will reduce sales admin means that salespeople will save an hour a day. It's unlikely that the sales force will be reduced, it's just that they have an hour more each day to be doing what you employ them to do – sell – and that's a benefit that you can express in money terms.

✓ **Non-quantifiable benefit:** As the name suggests, you can't express this benefit in money terms, at least not meaningfully. The benefit may be very worthwhile, though. An example is staff working conditions. If the project improves the factory or office environment, then that's worthwhile. But what's it worth in money terms? Can you prove that people who may otherwise have left will now stay, for example? Sometimes you can measure a part of this, such as productivity, but it's a tricky area, and generally you accept the benefit as important but non-quantifiable.

Don't ignore non-quantifiable benefits. Things like quality improvements can be hard or impossible to quantify, but they may be extremely important.

Now for a warning in the other direction. Be careful with non-quantifiable benefits and try hard to be realistic about them. Because you can never prove them, you need to be all the more careful that you're not fooling yourself about the existence and significance of non-quantifiable benefits.

Being prudent with benefit projections

A well-established accounting principle is that of being prudent. Being cautious and erring on the safe side is a well known trait of most accountants and the source of a lot of accountant jokes. You'd do well to follow the accountants' example when considering project benefits, though. Two very strong reasons exist to err on the safe side and, if anything, slightly understate the benefits rather than overstate them:

- **Perceptions of success and failure:** If your project delivers slightly more benefit than projected, everyone will think it's a particular success. If the project delivers less than projected, then people may see even a great project as a failure.

- **Incorrect strategy decisions:** If you overstate the benefits, the project may be run when it shouldn't be. That will have a double impact. The first is that the project won't be the good investment everyone thought it would be; second, it may well mean that the organisation didn't run, or delayed, another project that would have delivered worthwhile benefit.

Understanding benefits realisation

Benefits realisation is one of those terms that's caught on as management speak, and it's the one to use at important meetings to make it sound like you're at the very forefront of current management thinking. However, like many, but not quite all, management catchphrases, some value is tucked away inside the phrase. Put simply, benefits realisation is saying when you're going to see the benefits and how you're going to measure the benefits that you can quantify to demonstrate that they were forthcoming.

A common misunderstanding is that you see benefits only after the end of the project. In fact, you can see benefits at three places in the process, and you need to put plans in place to measure and report benefits at those points:

- ✔ **During the project:** In some projects, particularly but not solely business projects, deliverables are taken into operational use right through the project, and there isn't just one big delivery at the end. If things are being taken into operational use during the project, it's likely that you'll start to see benefits during the project too. You can and should measure these benefits and report them straight away to give confidence that the project is on track to deliver the benefits that justified running it.

- ✔ **At the end of the project:** You may see some benefits at the end of the project after the final delivery. For example, as soon you commission a the new machine at the end of a project, an immediate drop in maintenance costs follows over an old machine that needed daily attention.

- ✔ **After the end of the project:** Where you introduce something new, it's often the case that it takes a while for everything to settle down so that you can make an accurate measurement of the benefits. For example, with a new business procedure, staff work more slowly than usual when it's first introduced because they're still learning the procedure and it's unfamiliar. After a few weeks, performance picks up to what's now a normal level, so you can accurately measure and report the cost savings over the old procedure.

You can include your plans for measuring benefits in the Business Case itself or, particularly in larger projects where benefits realisation is often more complex, in a separate plan.

Avoiding benefits contamination

Benefits contamination is a term coined by Inspirandum when giving guidance on benefits realisation and, in particular, deciding how the benefits should be measured. The danger is that benefits are claimed for the project which are really due to something else. If you weren't quite the good Project Manager that you are, you might have been tempted to think that extra benefits are quite good and will make your project seem better. However, being both intelligent and thoroughly professional, as *For Dummies* readers are, you'll be quick to realise that such contamination is dangerous. It means that measures of what the project has actually achieved are inaccurate; worse still, contamination may lead to the organisation running more similar projects on the assumption that they'll also show this imaginary benefit.

In setting up benefits measures, you need mechanisms that will isolate benefits and directly link them to the project. That's harder than it sounds and sometimes needs very careful thought. It does no harm at all to get some help when thinking this through, and indeed it's a mark of professionalism to call in some help if you need it to get the Business Case right. In the case of benefits measures and avoiding benefits contamination, some input from a finance manager can be particularly helpful.

Writing the Business Case

When you are actually producing the Business Case, the format depends on who it's aimed at and your plan for the content. You can keep the Business Case very short and factual. However, if others have got to look at it for information or perhaps to approve it, then you may need to add some explanation. If you do include more information, keep your target audience in mind:

- ✔ **Keep it simple.** However, don't talk down to your readers. You need to assess where they're at and then write at that level.

- ✔ **Consider appendices.** If the fine financial detail isn't of interest to the bulk of your readers, consider putting an outline in the main part of the Business Case and having an appendix with the full data.

- ✔ **Spell out the benefits.** What may seem obvious to you may not be so obvious to people outside that area or to senior managers at the top of the organisation.

If you have to put information forward in a set format for financial approval, try not to separate that work out from the project's Business Case and so end up doing the work twice. Instead, adjust the Business Case format to fit the approval submission, put any extra information needed for the project into appendices, and then don't include the appendices in the copy that goes to the finance committee.

A membership example

A professional organisation in the UK has a membership and runs exams that are recognised worldwide. It wants to grow, because a bigger membership means a more secure future – it has competitors – and also that it can offer better services to its members. So it ran a project with the objective of increasing membership. So how do you know whether the project was successful? What was the measurable benefit?

✔ **Increased membership:** Ah, so membership has increased has it, but at what cost?

✔ **Increased membership at a reasonable cost:** That's better, after you define *reasonable*. However, what if membership increased but no more than that of competitive organisations that didn't run any membership projects at all – it was just natural growth in the market, and the project made no difference at all?

✔ **Increased membership 5 per cent above the market norm:** So, better still. But what if people are joining for other reasons, such as word-of-mouth recommendations, that have nothing to do with the project?

✔ **Increased membership linked to a project action:** The application form could include a 'why are you joining' question with options that relate directly and specifically to project activity.

Going Back to the Scope

Having set down the justification and benefits, it's time to revisit the scope to check it in two ways:

✔ To challenge the scope

✔ To see whether you need to add anything

In both cases, you work within any set constraints unless you think that you need to challenge such constraints and you're in a position to do that. You won't be able to challenge things like changes in the VAT rate, but you may well be in a position to challenge a constraint that you must use a particular brand of equipment, if new equipment has come onto the market from a different manufacturer that's cheaper to buy, technically more advanced and much easier to maintain.

Challenging the existing scope

For each area of the project, systematically check whether it's really worth doing or whether you could cut it out. For some things, the considerable project effort needed to include something simply isn't worthwhile given the very limited benefits that will result.

When challenging the scope, do bear in mind that some things are necessary even though they won't directly produce benefits (see the earlier section 'Understanding project justification' for examples).

Going the second mile

Keeping within the main thrust of the project, could you add anything usefully to the project to deliver extra benefit? It may be that you're already doing a substantial amount of work and by adding just a very small amount of additional functionality you could get considerably better benefits. This step isn't to encourage scope creep but rather to get the maximum possible value from the project.

In the UK, a stationery supply company put in a system to deal with customer orders and hold the data needed for that. The company wondered whether the system could serve any other purpose. The company realised that the data gave it valuable information, so extended its system to print personalised front pages to stick onto the front of mailed catalogues. So, if a customer buys a laminator for covering card and paper with plastic, but not the plastic pockets, on the next catalogue the customer sees on the front page: 'You haven't yet ordered laminating pouches from us. On page 5 you'll see that the A4 pouches are £5 a pack, but quote code XXX for your special price of £4.50.' The added functionality for the system led to significant extra sales based on a small amount of processing of data that the company had to hold in any case.

Getting to Grips with Techniques

A few techniques can help with Business Cases. The remainder of this chapter explains two, including cost–benefit analysis. For more detail on project techniques, you can look on the Internet or in specialised publications such as *The Project Techniques Toolbox*, written by Nick Graham and published by Inspirandum.

Calculating return on investment

The *return on investment* (ROI) is a simple division of the quantifiable benefits by the project cost in a stated period. Perhaps the project will cost £1 million but will lead to £5 million of benefits.

5,000,000/1,000,000 = ROI of 5

This ROI figure is useful but remember that the project may have important non-quantifiable benefits and the benefits projections may not be 100 per cent accurate in any case. To make the ROI figure meaningful, you should also state the time needed before the return; this has been called *the dollar day*. Investing £1 million and getting a return of £5 million within one year is very different from having to wait ten years for the same return.

Understanding cost–benefit analysis

Cost–benefit analysis is the most widely used technique for project Business Cases. The technique may sound complicated, but really it's very simple. You set down the costs of the project and compare them with the savings or benefits over a period of five years or so to see when the project will pay back or break even.

From Figure 3-1 you can see that the project is run in Year 0 and will pay back during Year 2. It will have offset the costs of the project and in fact will show a slight gain of £10,000 by the end of that year. Great: by the end of Year 2 we're already making money.

Allowing for inflation

The *direct payback* or *break-even model* is useful but it leaves out an important factor: future money isn't as valuable as today's money. If (and please note carefully the *if*) I offered you

£5,000 and asked whether you'd like it today or whether you'd prefer the £5,000 in five years' time, what would you reply? Well, 'Today!', without doubt and for two reasons. The first is you'd prefer to get your hands on the cash while I'm still feeling generous. The second is that in five years' time the money won't be as valuable: it won't have the same spending power.

£ '000s	Year 0	Year 1	Year 2	Year 3
Costs				
Equipment	105			
Project teams	135			
Maintenance	0	5	5	5
Total costs	240	5	5	5
Benefits				
Saved maintenance		15	15	20
Higher productivity		35	35	35
Increased order value		80	80	80
Total costs	0	130	130	135
Balance	−240	125	125	130
Cash flow	−240	−115	10	140

Figure 3-1: The direct payback model.

The further you go into the future, the less valuable money becomes. What you need to do in order to have a more realistic view is to discount the value of future money; the further you go into the future, the more you need to discount it.

Using discount factors – net present value

Depending on the current state of the economy and things like the rate of inflation, the discount factor varies. Ask your finance people what the current factor is or check on the Internet. Figure 3-2 uses a discount rate of 5 per cent so at Year 0, £1 is worth £1. By Year 3, though, £1 is only worth 86.4 pence. You express future money in today's values.

If you use a spreadsheet, you'll find a function that deals with discounts – *NPV*, which stands for net present value.

Using the same example as before, Figure 3-2 now shows that the project doesn't actually break even in Year 2 at all; by the end of that year, it's still £3,000 down. In fact, break-even occurs in Year 3, and the overall benefits are lower too.

Although it gives a more accurate view, discounted cash flow is still limited so don't get too carried away:

- ✔ It assumes that the economy will remain stable for the period covered by the cash flow, and so uses a uniform discount value over the period.

- ✔ It assumes that the projected benefits will be forthcoming and projections of costs for the future years are accurate.

- ✔ It doesn't account for non-quantifiable benefits, of which some or all may be extremely important.

£ '000s	Year 0	Year 1	Year 2	Year 3
Costs				
Equipment	105			
Project teams	135			
Maintenance	0	5	5	5
Total costs	240	5	5	5
Benefits				
Saved maintenance		15	15	20
Higher productivity		35	35	35
Increased order value		80	80	80
Total costs	0	130	130	135
Balance	−240	125	125	130
Cash flow	−240	−115	10	140
5% discount factor				
Discount factor	1.000	0.952	0.907	0.864
Discounted balance	−240	119	118	117
Discounted cash flow	−240	−121	−3	114

Figure 3-2: Discounted cash flow.

Chapter 4

Knowing the Stakeholders

*O*ften a project is like an iceberg: nine-tenths of it lurks below the surface. You receive an assignment and you think you know what it entails and who needs to be involved. Then, as the project unfolds, new people emerge who may affect your goals and your approach to the project.

Dick Parris, an experienced Project Manager and trainer, has a favourite expression: 'Projects are about people.' Dick's right. You can have a great project idea, be implementing the latest whiz-bang technology, and use a great project methodology, but if you don't get the people side right, you run a very real risk of failure.

On the inside of the project are the people involved in project management and then the teams that are actually doing the work. You need these people to be enthusiastic and empowered (check out Chapters 11 and 12 for more). Then, on the outside, you have a wide array of people with an interest in the project, and who can often make or break it.

Unless your project is one of a small minority that only really affects you and your immediate staff, you need to carefully consider the various stakeholders. This chapter helps you establish who the stakeholders are, what their view of the project is, whether to involve them in some way and, if you do need to involve them, how. It also has a few hints and tips on handling any stakeholders who are opposed to your project and who may not be afraid of saying so.

Managing Stakeholders

The area of project work you're involved in with stakeholders is called, not surprisingly, *stakeholder management*. Although that term has become a buzzword, don't dismiss it, because this part of project management can ultimately hold the key to success or failure in your project.

A *stakeholder* can be any person or group that supports, is affected by or is interested in your project. Project stakeholders may be located inside your organisation or outside, or both. In addition to making sure that your project has maximum support, knowing who the stakeholders are helps you to:

- Consider whether, when and how to involve them

- Understand your project communication needs

- Determine whether the reach and impact of the project is bigger or smaller than you originally anticipated

You risk compromising your project in two ways when you don't involve key people or groups in your project, and in a timely manner:

- You may miss important information that can affect the project's performance and ultimate success.

- Usually more painful, you may upset someone. And you can be sure that when people feel slighted or insulted – or just plain overlooked – they're more likely to oppose your project than become wildly enthusiastic supporters.

Do stakeholder problems mean you should give up immediately? No, of course not. But such people issues do mean that in order to be successful you need to manage the 'soft' people side of the project as well as the 'hard' skills side that includes things like planning.

Identifying stakeholders

Identifying stakeholders can simply mean that you sit down and think through the project and its environs, but it's often useful to talk to other people in the project who may think of people or groups that don't immediately spring to your mind.

Developing a Stakeholder List

As you identify the different stakeholders in your project, you may find it helpful to record them in the form of a *Stakeholder List*. As you develop your Communications Management Plan (covered in detail in Chapter 14), for example, you can quickly scan the list to make sure you haven't left anyone out.

A Stakeholder List is a living document. You can start developing your list as soon as you begin thinking about your project, rather than risk forgetting them. When you discuss your project with other people, ask them who they think may be affected by or interested in your project.

Using categories

To help ensure that you include all appropriate people, you may find it sensible to structure your list with categories.

You can work out your categories, but here's one example:

- ✔ **Internal:** People and groups inside your organisation:

    - **End users:** People who'll use the things that the project will produce

    - **Groups needed just for this project:** Teams and individuals with special, often technical, knowledge related to this project

- **Requesters:** The person who came up with the idea for your project, and all the people through whom the request passed before you received it

- **Senior management:** Executive-level management responsible for the general oversight of all organisational operations

- **Specialist interests:** Groups typically involved in most projects in the organisation, such as the human resources, finance, contracts and legal departments

- **Team members:** People assigned to the project, whose work the Project Manager directs

✔ **External:** People and groups outside your organisation:

- **Business partners:** Groups or organisations with which you may pursue joint ventures including, perhaps, this project

- **Clients or customers:** People or groups that buy or use your organisation's products or services

- **Professional societies:** Groups of professionals that may influence or be interested in your project

- **Regulators:** Government and agencies that establish regulations and guidelines that govern some aspect of your project work

- **Staff associations and unions:** Partly because they can often make valuable contributions to the project, but also because they may get direct enquiries from staff about it and need information to respond

- **The public:** The local, national and international community of people who may be affected by or interested in your project

- **The media:** If your project is in the public spotlight, the media can have a strong influence on people's perception of your project, good or bad

- **Vendors, suppliers and contractors:** Organisations that provide staff, raw materials, equipment or other resources required to perform your project's work

Spotlighting senior management

All of the interest groups in the preceding list are important, but a particularly important one is senior management. Surveys of project failure show that a very common cause of problems is lack of senior management buy-in. If your project is anything other than small or is going outside the boundaries of your own work area, you must do your very best to secure this buy-in. Otherwise, senior management is likely to undermine your efforts on the project, such as by seeing the project as unimportant and transferring staff or funds to other areas part way through. Such undermining often happens because the senior managers were never seriously committed to the project in the first place.

Many project methodologies, including PRINCE2 and PRIME have senior management representation on the project management team (senior, that is, relative to the project), and usually in the powerful position of having ultimate responsibility for the project. That representation and structure is no coincidence and helps lock in senior management commitment to the project.

Considering areas that are often overlooked

As you develop your Stakeholder List, be particularly careful to think through the following areas, because they're easy to overlook:

- ✔ **End users of your project's products:** Involving end users at the beginning and throughout your project helps ensure that the products and services delivered by the project will work successfully.

  In some cases you don't know who the end users are, such as potential buyers of a new retail product. Instead, choose people who understand and represent the interests of those end users, such as sales and marketing staff.

- ✔ **People who'll maintain or support the final product:** Involving these people throughout your project gives them a chance to make your project's products easier to maintain. It also allows them to become familiar with the products and prepare for the future maintenance.

✔ **Support staff:** Support areas include finance, legal, HR (Human Resources) and the Project Office if you have one. If support staff know about your project early, they can fit you into their work schedules more readily. They can also tell you information about their capabilities and processes that may influence what your project can accomplish and by when.

Specialists, such as legal specialists, prefer to be involved early on so that they can check that things are right and give you a steer if needed. Involving specialists early on is much better than not consulting them but then calling for them later in a flat panic because you've encountered serious legal problems and need the specialists to put in huge effort to dig you out of the mess. If you think that your project may have a legal dimension, put your organisation's legal advisers on your Stakeholder List.

Keeping the Stakeholder List up to date

As the project develops, you may well discover more people who have a genuine interest in it. Keep the Stakeholder List up to date and then review it periodically to see how you need to keep people informed and how you need to involve them.

If you need to develop a Stakeholder List for most of your projects, consider setting up a template that contains typical categories and stakeholders. Using a template can save you time and improve your accuracy.

Analysing the stakeholders

Stakeholder analysis is considering each stakeholder to ask where she is with the project – frequently in the two dimensions of degree of influence and then her positive or negative view of the project. You may set out to actively change the position or outlook of certain stakeholders, but to do that you clearly need to establish first where they are now.

Developing a Stakeholder Matrix

The Stakeholder Matrix is a simple idea, but a powerful one because it helps you see where stakeholders are in terms of their support of the project and the degree of influence over it. It helps you consider where you need to try to change that position. Figure 4-1 marks in four people as examples, suggesting four different approaches.

1. This person is neither for nor against the project and has medium influence over it. Your priority is to make this person much more positive about the project and then, if you succeed, you can move on to try and make the person more influential.

2. This person is a project champion, very much in favour of the project, and is also in a position of significant influence. Be careful how you think about people in this area of the matrix. An initial reaction may be that you don't need to do anything, but actually you must work to make sure that they stay on-side and enthusiastic.

3. The third person is really for your project but doesn't have much influence. The question for this person is whether you do something to increase her influence and so make her support more effective.

4. Here is the opposition, and quite serious opposition too. Not only is the person firmly against your project but she also has a high degree of influence. You need to work to convince her that the project is worthwhile and so get her support. If you're a more political player, you might also be looking to see whether you can reduce this person's influence.

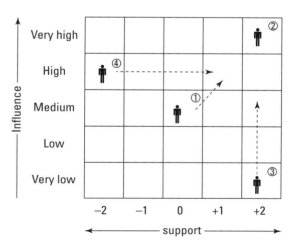

Figure 4-1: The Stakeholder Matrix.

Although the matrix is extremely useful in getting a picture of where individual stakeholders are, it's also useful for seeing the overall distribution. For example, you may see that the majority of the stakeholders are in favour of your project but that relatively few of them are in a position of influence.

If you want to, you can also make the matrix more sophisticated by showing the position of stakeholders before any management action, and your assessment of their position after management action is in place.

Understanding the positions

Before you can try to maintain or change a stakeholder's position, you need to understand why a person or group has taken a particular stance.

Understanding a negative stance

When someone has objections to the project, it's important to hear those objections. And *hearing* means working hard to understand and trying to see things from the stakeholder's position. In some cases, those making the objections reduce their opposition when they feel that they've at least been heard rather than just plain ignored.

Another reason for a negative stance is lack of understanding about the project, or even misunderstanding. Sometimes they're scared to commit, because they aren't sure exactly what they're committing to.

Understanding a positive stance

If a stakeholder has a positive stance then, perhaps strangely, you also need to understand why. You can't protect a position until you know the underlying reasons for it. The stakeholder may be a massive fan of your project because it will deal with a problem that's plagued her staff for years. If the project comes under pressure of time and budget, and the plan shows that you need to reduce the scope, you'd do well to think twice before cutting the part that deals with that stakeholder's problem.

Deciding action

Your stakeholder management now moves clearly from the analysis part into the action part as you consider *what* you need to do. On the one hand, you may want to consolidate a stakeholder's current position to make sure, for example, that the person stays enthusiastic and on-side. On the other hand, you may want to try and change the stakeholder's position, particularly if it's currently against the project.

Looking at the possibilities

Your responsibility as a Project Manager is to deliver the project. What you can't afford is to manage your stakeholders superbly but fail in that project delivery. So you have to balance out stakeholder management. Exactly what effort is needed and how much work can be justified?

Involving others

Don't think that working with stakeholders is all down to you as a Project Manager. If you have more senior managers involved in the project, perhaps on a project steering committee or as sponsors, talk to them about stakeholder issues. They may be better placed than you to take the agreed actions and so be much more effective.

Working with stakeholders

Having decided that you need to involve some of the stakeholders, or at least communicate information to them, you need to decide *how* best to do that. Think about:

- **Approval:** Before completing the project, you may need to get approval from stakeholders who have authority to make decisions.

- **Communication:** How you'll communicate information such as on the impact the project will have, its progress and benefits projections.

- **Consultation:** Do you need to get agreement from stakeholders at particular points in the project? How will you do that or, if you're constrained by procedures, how must you do that?

✔ **Participation:** When making organisational change, you get people on-side more easily if you involve them in the change process, so how will you do that? For example, you may get operational staff involved to help design new procedures. That helps ensure that the procedures work but also that the operational staff 'own' them from the outset.

Linking with communications

A lot of the stakeholder management actions relate to communications. It follows that as you think about the stakeholders, you adjust the Communications Management Plan. In medium to large projects particularly, consider:

✔ **Briefings:** Such as a lunchtime 20-minute illustrated talk once a month

✔ **News sheet:** An illustrated project bulletin circulated to everyone with an interest in the project

✔ **Roadshow:** Going around to the regional offices before the product launch

✔ **Website:** A dedicated website for the project, with news and progress information, excluding anything sensitive

Use these strategies with care because they take effort, but one or more may be a really effective way of communicating information to important stakeholders.

Planning the work

Some work to manage stakeholders is effectively continuous, such as keeping everyone up to speed with progress and new developments on the project. Other work focuses on particular points. You need to think through your own project, come up with your own requirements, and then build the actions into the plan at the appropriate points.

Handling Opposition

If one or more people are dead set against your project, then you won't need this book to tell you that you've got problems. However, although serious, such problems aren't insurmountable; this section gives a bit more help.

Before reading on, check out the 'Understanding positions' section, earlier in the chapter. People rarely take action or hold a position without a reason, no matter how valid or invalid you think that reason is. Try hard to find out why a person is opposing your project.

Solving the problems

If people are opposed to your project because it will cause genuine problems, do your best to make adjustments so that the project won't cause problems. Remember that sometimes objections are valid. Taking this approach can result in a win–win; you avoid the problems, and the people who raised the objections are now really impressed that you listened and then worked with them to solve the difficulties.

Focusing on the common areas

Try to identify common areas and major on what you have in common, not on points that divide, especially if those points are minor. Sometimes people lose all sense of proportion when making negative arguments. Minor issues that are mole-hills assume the proportions of mountains and then obscure nearly everything else.

Realising that you're a threat

When looking for underlying reasons for a negative stance, consider the idea that people are probably seeing you, your project, or both, as a threat. Projects, by definition, are usually changing something, and generally people don't like change. You may not notice people's dislike of change at first because:

- You probably like change or else you wouldn't be involved with projects. It's natural enough to think that other people see the project the way you do, so you may be puzzled as to why they don't share your enthusiasm.

- 'Operation cover-up' is underway. If a managing director promotes a project at the company meeting by saying it will 'change the face of our whole operation', everyone may clap and smile and say 'wonderful idea' to each other, while saying secretly to themselves 'over my dead body!'

You need, then, to reduce the threat. Try the following:

- ✔ **Be scrupulously honest.** One thing guaranteed to heighten threat and fear is distortion. People need to know that when you say something, it's true. That way they learn to trust you instead of the rumour mill.

- ✔ **Be open.** Make as much known about the project as possible. If people think you're hiding things, they imagine all sorts of nasty threatening reasons why. That's completely unnecessary if the information wasn't secret in the first place.

- ✔ **Act open.** It's surprising how little things can increase or decrease the feeling of threat. If you're talking to someone and want to take notes, ask her permission, even if she's very junior. The person is highly unlikely to say no, but the act of asking gives her the feeling of being in control, which runs counter to feeling threatened. Also, ask if you can send her a copy afterwards to check that you've got the details right. Again, all of this signals openness, which does a lot to play down threat.

- ✔ **Involve people as much as you can.** Involvement is a key component in change management, and your project is about change. Nobody likes things being imposed on them, and a hugely different dynamic exists where people are involved.

- ✔ **Understand the extent and strength of opposition.** Use techniques such as Force Field Analysis to model the forces at play so you can understand them and the overall dynamic of the project better. You can find information on this technique in publications like Inspirandum's *The Project Techniques Toolbox,* by Nick Graham.

Overriding the opposition

Well, that's it for the kind stuff; now on to the tough stuff. If you have serious opposition but the project must get done, you need to stamp on the opposition. Such stamping presupposes that you've done everything possible to win over the opposing stakeholders.

As a Project Manager, you probably won't have the personal authority to do much stamping! Even if you're a fairly high grade, the chances are that your project is cross-functional and the opposition is coming from another department where you don't have any authority. The answer in this case is to go higher. For example, work with your project sponsor to get the managing director to issue a notice saying that this project is going ahead and that she requires staff in all departments to cooperate to ensure that the project is successful. Now if anyone opposes you or the project, they put themselves in opposition to the management board.

Don't stamp unless you really, really need to and all else has failed. After you've got heavy, you'll almost certainly have eliminated any further possibility of winning people over. The cooperation you do now get is likely to be half-hearted, and the bad feeling it creates will last long after the end of the project.

Part II
Building the Plans

In this part . . .

You have the greatest chance of achieving project success when you have a good plan that shows it's possible to accomplish everything on time, to budget and to the right level of quality.

This part explains the very powerful 'product led' approach to planning, how to do activity planning and then resource planning, including the finances. And last, but definitely not least, it shows how you can identify and deal with potential project risks.

Chapter 5

Planning with Deliverables First

- -

- -

*I*f you've been around projects for a while and come across other books or used project management software (actually it's usually only scheduling software), you've seen the planning approach in which you first list all the activities or tasks for a project and then draw up a Gantt Chart with its familiar horizontal bars (see Chapter 6 for more on this chart). To help you get to your task list, you may also have used a hierarchical diagram in which you can break down the major activities into more detail to determine a working list of tasks.

This chapter, however, starts the planning up front of the activities: it starts with thinking about, understanding and defining what you need to deliver. Then, when you're as clear as you can be on what you're going to deliver, you can start thinking through what activities you need to build those deliverables.

This chapter makes the case for the *product-led* or *product-based* approach to planning and also gives you some extremely powerful techniques. The product-led approach is logical, and it's hard to overstate just how very good it is. Not only is it an enormous help in planning, but it also opens the door to particularly effective quality management and progress control.

The product-led approach to planning isn't intuitive, so you may need some time to get your head around it. If you're reading this book because you're completely new to project management, then you'll be delighted to know that you'll probably find the technique fairly straightforward and easy to use. If you're a more experienced Project Manager, you may take to the product-led approach easily too, but don't be worried if you have a bit of a struggle, and don't give up, because the benefits of product-led planning hugely repay your efforts in getting to grips with the approach. Keep at it and suddenly you find everything clicks into place; after that, planning with products will seem easy and it will simply become the way you think and work.

Seeing the Logic

You can't really argue with the logic of the product-led approach. How can you possibly determine activities and time durations with any accuracy if you're unclear about what it is you're going to build?

Many approaches to project management refer to deliverables as *products*. What you produce are the products.

Thinking 'product' first

To show the logic of looking at deliverables, or products, first, the following example follows the process of activity-led planning to show where it can create some problems.

Okay, we're working on a project and our computer software tells us to list the activities first. We write on our list 'Build the wall', because that's going to be an important element in this project, which involves some alterations to our headquarters building. After we've entered this and the other tasks, the next step is to draw bars on a Gantt Chart to indicate the time duration. Please say then, how long it takes to build a wall.

You probably want to start asking questions about the wall, such as how high it will be and how long, and the sort of finish required. But you missed the question and aren't helping. The software says that step two is to enter the time duration, not start a debate, so please give your estimate. How long does it take to build a wall?

Who's using product-led planning?

The product-led approach is in increasing use, but not always to its full extent. In its PMBOK (*Project Management Body of Knowledge*), the American Project Management Institute (PMI) refers to products as a key focus. NASA, the American space agency, developed a product-based approach and in a guidance paper on Work Breakdown Structures, available on the NASA website, you see that, for the most part, the structure shows products. Some academic bodies working in the field of project management have developed the product approach, and although they've re-invented the wheel in some cases, they've helped establish the technique. Product-led planning is also built into some project methodologies such as PRIME, where it's a key focus, and PRINCE2, which expects you to use the product-led approach.

It's worth commenting briefly on PRINCE2 because it's in such widespread use. The method is a little strange because in the latest manual edition (2009), the implementation has been rolled back, taking out some of the useful refinements developed for an earlier edition. The new manual also describes the very powerful progress-monitoring element of product planning as 'optional' and confuses how you should carry out progress monitoring. Why those responsible for the method should want to abandon useful refinements is something of a mystery. If you're using PRINCE2 and want to know more about how to incorporate product planning without losing its power, you might like to buy a copy of *PRINCE2 For Dummies* by Nick Graham (Wiley).

The example shows a significant problem when you start planning with the activities. Activities are a comfortable place to start, but not a logical place. The comfort comes because people normally think *activity* when faced with a project. 'Oh, I need to do this, and I must remember to do that.' It's do, do, do. But how can you accurately determine the activities needed to build a brick wall and how long they're likely to take unless you've first defined what it is you mean by *brick wall*. So, you were right to want to ask questions.

The sorts of questions that you may think about are:

ム How long is the wall and how high? The height is significant because we'll need scaffolding if the wall is higher than about 2 metres.

✔ When you say *wall*, does that include the foundations?

✔ Where's the wall going to be? If it's at the front of the building and in full public view, it needs to be neatly finished, but if it's a supporting wall that'll be covered by an earth bank, we can leave it rough.

✔ Will the wall be one brick deep or two?

✔ If the wall is in public view, is it to be plain brick, Flemish bond or some intricate design with the company logo in 3D?

Whatever the product, you need to define and understand it so that you can determine what tasks you need to do to create the product and how long those tasks will take.

If you're already deeply into activity-driven approaches, your response may well be that you do this sort of thinking already. If you do respond like that, great, because you're already halfway there. The product-led approach just emphasises that line of thinking and gives you some particularly powerful techniques to help.

Understanding the problems of an activity focus

Please note carefully that taking a product-led approach doesn't do away with activity planning. Activity planning is powerful and isn't only advantageous but also absolutely essential. But product planning provides a very logical and powerful front end. Starting instead with activities brings two problems:

✔ Until you have a clear idea of what you need to build, you aren't going to have a clear idea of the activities needed and are highly likely to miss some out. In turn, that means that you're likely to underestimate the effort and time needed for the project, which, indeed, is a very common cause of project problems.

✔ Even where you correctly identify activities, time estimates are likely to be wrong. Returning to the example of the task to build a wall that we use in the previous section, clearly a great deal of difference exists between the time needed to build a small garden wall and the time needed to build something on the scale of the Great Wall of China.

Many projects, encouraged by books and software, plunge into activity planning without proper thought about what is to be produced. It's no wonder then that estimates of time and cost are inaccurate and the project is then plagued with problems where essential work is identified during the project that isn't on the plan. Many time sheets built into project scheduling software have a section for 'Unscheduled activity' where project staff can report work they're having to do that wasn't foreseen. Such problems lead to projects being late in delivery and overspent on budget.

Knowing What a Product Is – and Isn't

There are a few refinements on what products are, but the starting point is simple. A *product* is something that one of your project teams (that may be just one person) builds. When a team leader comes up to you and says, 'We've finished it, here it is,' what is *it*? A product is something that you can hold in your hand or, if it's too big for that, walk up and kick.

Products in your projects might include:

- ✔ Brick wall – you can kick it

- ✔ Computer program – you can print it out and hold it

- ✔ Decorated room – you can stamp around it and kick the walls, though try not to dirty the new paint

- ✔ Instruction manual – you can hold it

Things that aren't products, but are commonly mistaken for them, are:

- ✔ Designers – that's a staff resource. The designers are the people who create your product 'Office design document'. Unless your project is quite long and rather exciting, you won't be making people!

- ✔ Money – that's a resource. Unless you work for the Royal Mint or your own country's equivalent, actually producing money is illegal and you can spend years in prison for it, causing substantial project delay.

- Jobsworth Office Furnishings Ltd – that's a source of supply. The products are likely to be desks and chairs, and Jobsworth Office Furnishings Ltd is where you bought them.

- Walls built – that's a point in time when the walls have all been built. You don't kick 'walls built'; instead the products that you kick are 'built walls' – or more simply 'walls', because if they aren't built, then they aren't walls.

- Writing programs – that's a task or activity; notice the verb *write*.

Finding Good Product Names

As you think about your project's products, you may come up with better and more appropriate names for some of them. In the bullet point above, if you're particularly fast-thinking, you may have said to yourself that 'Jobsworth Office Furnishings Ltd' might well be a product if the project includes setting up the company. That's true, but then the product name isn't a particularly good one. The product that you hold in your hand isn't going to be the company, but rather something like 'company registration document'. As you work through the products, you're likely to think of better, more descriptive names for some – so change them.

Good and bad product names

Here's a snapshot of some great and rubbish product names:

- **28** – bad because you don't know what product 28 is without looking it up

- **Fully detailed specification of the engineering operations procedure** – bad; it's too long

- **New user manual** – good; it's short and descriptive

- **15. Approved design** – good; it's short, descriptive and has a reference to its Product Definition – number 15.

Product names should be short and descriptive. Later on you'll be drawing up some diagrams, and you need short names to go into the boxes on the diagrams. If you have long, unwieldy names, you'll be tempted to use numbers instead, and that can cause problems.

Where you're working on a project that involves other people, which is usual, then stick to the terminology in use in their part of the organisation. If the engineering staff refer to something as the 'upgrade plan' and in your diagrams you call the product 'modification schedule', the engineers won't recognise the product and won't be able to say whether the diagrams are correct. Stay with their names and note down separately the definition of them if it's not obvious to you from the product titles.

Using a Business Project Example

This part of the chapter uses an example to show how the product-planning sequence works. The example is a small business project to review and improve a business process in an accounts department, including a small update to some computer software.

Identifying the products

In the project example to review and adjust an accounts procedure, the initial products – just in the order they come to mind – are:

- ✔ **Problems and requirements list:** A list of things that the staff say are causing difficulties with the present way of doing things, and their wish list for how they would like a new one to work

- ✔ **Updated computer system:** Adjusted to deal with any changes decided on in the revised procedure

✔ **Draft of new accounts procedure:** An outline of the intended new approach

✔ **Final new procedure design:** The agreed new procedure and the one that will be implemented

✔ **Training plan:** A list of staff who need to be trained in the revised procedure and what they need to know

✔ **Training course:** The short course of two to three hours to explain the new procedures to staff

✔ **New accounts procedure:** The implemented new procedure, complete with the upgrade to the computer

For your projects, you can make up a product list from your own knowledge if you already know the business area, but even then you'll probably want to involve some other people to check that the list is correct. If you don't know the project at all, don't worry. You can do this work in a workshop format and facilitate the product planning by briefly explaining the product-planning approach and then guiding the session.

Some techniques can help bring some structure into your thinking about products – see the later section 'Using a Structured Product List'. For now, it's enough to work with a simple list.

Developing a sequence

The next step is powerful; seriously powerful. You develop a very simple sequence diagram. This is called a Work Flow Diagram or sometimes a Product Flow Diagram.

The Work Flow Diagram simply shows the products in the order that they will be created in the project. Figure 5-1 is a first attempt at the sequence.

Checking the Work Flow – bottom up

What comes next is the most important part of the activity in drawing a Work Flow Diagram. It's called the bottom-up check. Guess where you start on the diagram? Ah, well done, you're getting the hang of this rapidly.

You do two tests in the bottom-up check:

✔ For each dependency arrow, are you absolutely sure that you can't begin the later product until the earlier one is finished?

✔ To build a product, you've established that you need the products feeding into it. The next question is, do you need any products other than those already connected by an arrow? You may find that a dependency arrow is missing from another product already on the diagram or, very commonly, you discover one or more new products that aren't on the diagram at all at the moment.

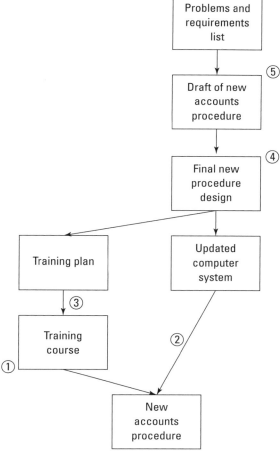

Figure 5-1: Work Flow Diagram – first attempt.

Five locations are labelled on the first attempt at a Work Flow Diagram in Figure 5-1. These mark some problems that you discover in the bottom-up check:

1. You realise that 'Training course' isn't very good name. You can't hold a training course in your hand or kick it. A better product name is 'Trained accounts staff'. In the bottom-up check, you decide that it's correct that you need a training plan to produce the trained staff, so the dependency arrow is correct.

2. You realise that you also need the updated computer system for the training course. Unless that's available, the staff won't be properly trained because they won't have seen the changes and won't know how to work the changed system. The dependency from 'Updated computer system' to 'New accounts procedure' looked right at first, but now you see that you need to change the arrow to feed into the new 'Trained accounts staff' product. The trained staff also need sight of a new procedures manual for the training, which in turn can't be produced until the computer updates have been done so that screen shots can be included in the manual; so you discover a second missing product, 'Revised procedure manual'.

3. When you check the 'Trained accounts staff' (previously called 'Training course') product further, some thinking reveals that you don't just need a training plan, but also training materials. That's yet another new product that you need to put up front of the 'Trained accounts staff' product and after 'Training plan'.

4. It was clear that people would need to look at the draft design before it was finalised, but you now see that you need a formal response from some staff, such as your finance specialists, to confirm that the new procedure complies with the latest finance regulations. Because other staff comments really should be written down so that you can keep track of them and make sure they've all been considered, you identify a new product of 'Staff comments'. These comments are a product; they can be printed off and held in your hand.

5. Finally, on looking at the 'Draft of new accounts procedure', you see that the team will need a copy of the existing procedure manual to be sure they're clear on how things work at the moment in order to be able to correctly specify what the changes are.

The bottom-up check has discovered the missing products of Training materials, Current procedure manual, Revised procedure manual and Staff comments, and has also revealed that you need to change some dependencies.

Time for a re-draw of the Work Flow Diagram then – see Figure 5-2.

Seeing what's inside the project and what's outside

In Figure 5-2 you may have noticed that most products are in a rectangle but two are in ovals. The shapes discriminate between internal and external products. An *internal product* is product that will be developed by one of the project teams. An *external product* is one that won't be developed by a project team, although it may be a very important product. Two sources of external products exist:

> ✔ **Products that already exist** (like the Current procedure manual in Figure 5-2). If the product already exists at the start of the project, clearly a project team isn't going to build the product during the project.

> ✔ **Something supplied from people outside the project** (like the Staff comments in Figure 5-2). The product may be very important, but it won't be built by one of the project teams. In a computer project, it is unlikely that your organisation will build the computer, but it's a very important product and the project can't go ahead without it.

The ovals and rectangles make the project boundary clear. In Figure 5-2 the ovals are to the outside of the diagram – although it isn't always possible to do that – so the boundary is particularly clear and can be shown with a dashed line.

Sticking to a limit of 30 products

The number of boxes in the diagram should be between about 15 and about 30. If you go much beyond 30, the diagram gets too complicated and you find that you can't see anything; it all starts to look like a ball of string. In a small project, you have space to go into quite a lot of detail. If, however, your project is to review the business processes throughout John Wiley & Sons publishing worldwide (and no, we're not hinting, although project consultancy services are available from both authors at a very reasonable rate), then the project is so enormous that the 30 products will be quite chunky, to use a technical expression.

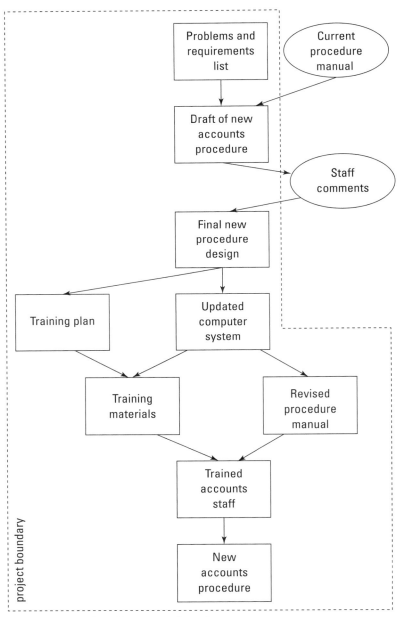

Figure 5-2: Work Flow Diagram – adjusted.

It's normal for a project to be coming up to the 30 limit quite nicely when the bottom-up check reveals big areas of the project that you hadn't realised were there, and you suddenly find that you have 50 products. The answer in that case is to combine some of the products and so show less detail in the diagram. Don't worry about combining products to stay within the limit. When you develop a more detailed stage plan later on for that part of the project, you can then show that greater level of detail. Chapter 8 has more on the levels of planning, including stage planning.

Where you have combined products, note down now what sub-products are contained in the new higher level one, so that you don't lose the more detailed thinking you've already done. You can note it on the Product Definition (see the section 'Defining the products'), and the information will be safe until you need to use it.

Using names, not numbers

It's extremely important to use names on the diagram and not numbers. If you replace text with numbers (perhaps because you've chosen very long product names), the diagram loses meaning. If you have to look up the product numbers, you'll only ever understand a part of the diagram at a time.

You're also likely to miss dependencies because you can't remember what all 30 product boxes are. Sooner or later you'll make a bad mistake, and sure as eggs is eggs, it'll be sooner.

The problem with numbers reinforces the point that you should find short, descriptive product names so that they fit easily into the boxes and so you won't be tempted to replace the names with numbers (see the earlier section 'Finding Good Product Names'). If you want to use numbers as well as names, that's fine, and actually an advantage because you can quickly look up the relevant Product Definition, as covered in the next section.

Defining the products

For each product on the diagram, you now write a Product Definition, sometimes known as a Product Description. Product Definition is really a better term because it includes a description but rather more besides.

Have you ever heard a conversation that included the words, 'Oh, I thought you meant . . .'? It's that sort of conversation, with the accompanying problems of wasted money and of project delay, that the Product Definition does so much to avoid.

The *Project Definition* simply defines what the product is and also includes information on the quality criteria it must satisfy and how it will be tested to make sure that it does meet them. As with the rest of product-led planning, the case for the Product Definition is logical. If you're going to ask a team or an individual to build something for you, you're going to have to define what it is.

You may find this simple list of headings useful as a default, but you can always alter the headings to suit your own particular organisation or even a specific project.

- ✔ **Reference:** A product number.

- ✔ **Author and date:** The person responsible for this particular Product Definition.

- ✔ **Description:** A textual description of the product.

- ✔ **Sub-products:** If this product is made up of any lower-level components.

- ✔ **Quality criteria:** What quality criteria must the product must satisfy to be acceptable?

- ✔ **Tests:** To ensure that the product meets its quality criteria.

- ✔ **Required resource:** What team hours, skills and costs you anticipate you need to build the product and to test it.

- ✔ **Responsibilities:** As you get into more detailed planning, you can enter the names of the people (or team) who'll be building the product and those who'll be testing it.

If you're using the PRINCE2 methodology, you'll find that it refers to this document as a Product Description; the content is slightly different, although the concept is the same. If you're working to PMI standards, you'll find that the product details are stored in what the PMI calls the Work Breakdown Structure (WBS) Dictionary. Although the PMI mixes information on tasks and products, the same underlying thinking is there – that you need to set down information on deliverables somewhere.

Taking the time to get the Project Definition right

In the UK, a large company asked Inspirandum to provide consultancy support to facilitate a product-planning workshop for a big, business-critical project to replace machines in an industrial environment. Six staff were flown in from overseas to take part in the workshop, and three more were from within the UK, then there was the Inspirandum consultant making ten in all. Part of that workshop was to produce Product Definitions for all the products. One Product Definition took four hours to produce with all ten people involved – that's 40 staff hours. What was the reaction of the participants at the end of the four hours do you think? That product planning is long winded? No, actually they were delighted. The project was extremely important and this particular product was absolutely vital, yet at the outset nobody really understood it. At the end of the four hours everyone understood the product and was agreed on exactly what it was. In a difficult, business-critical project that was going to last some 18 months, everyone thought that pinning this product down so precisely was 40 staff hours very well spent. In the same workshop, two staff produced a Product Definition for a less contentious product in just over ten minutes.

Using a Structured Product List

In the planning example used in the earlier section 'Using a Business Project Example', the initial list of products was compiled at random as products came to mind. In many projects, it can be a real help to use a bit of structure and think through the project in an orderly way, looking at different categories of product in turn.

For example, if the project is a house build, you might first list all the brickwork products, then all the electrical products, then woodwork products and finally decorating products. For the electrical products, you might find it easier still if you break that into two sub-categories and think first about the lighting circuit products and then the power circuit products.

Using categories provides some helpful structure and forms a hierarchy. You might write that down in the form of indented paragraphs. Taking just the first two of the four categories for the house build, the list might look like this:

Brickwork products

> Foundations

> Outer walls

> Garden wall

Electrical products

> Lighting circuit products

>> Lights

>> Switches

>> 5-amp lighting cabling

> Power circuit products

>> Fuse board (consumer unit)

>> 13-amp power cabling

>> Power sockets

If you like Mind Maps, you might prefer to list products using that format, which is essentially a hierarchy bent around in a circle. Again, you might prefer a hierarchy diagram such as that shown in Figure 5-3.

The hierarchy diagram is just like the indented list or Mind Map, only this time you show the categories and products in boxes. The advantage of this format is that you can use the same symbols as on the Work Flow Diagram (see the earlier section 'Developing a sequence') and show whether products are internal or external. Figure 5-3 uses the example of the new office procedure from the earlier section 'Using a Business Project Example'.

The bottom level of the Work Breakdown Structure hierarchy forms the list of products that you'll carry forward to the Work Flow Diagram. In Figure 5-3 a dashed line identifies the bottom level, with the products shown in grey, even though some products are physically higher up in the diagram. The key point is that there is nothing underneath each of the boxes along that dashed line, so those boxes are all bottom level no matter where they are physically. The top box on the diagram is the whole project, and that maps to the last box on the Work Flow Diagram.

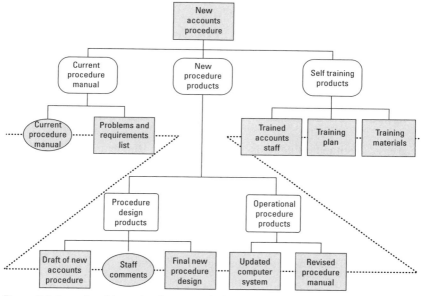

Figure 5-3: A product hierarchy diagram – the Work Breakdown Structure.

The grouping or category boxes, shown with a rounded rectangle symbol in Figure 5-3, are effectively headings and not products and so don't form part of the product list. The category boxes simply show why that set of products have been grouped together.

No rules exist about the groupings or categories; they're just what help you to think through the project systematically. In larger projects involving contracts, a common grouping is by contract. If the subject of the whole project is unfamiliar to you and you don't know what the high-level categories are, just go straight for the Work Flow Diagram and don't do the Work Breakdown Structure. The Work Flow Diagram is helpful in that case because it is a network diagram and you don't have to start at the top; you can start anywhere with the information you have.

Working at different levels of detail

This chapter focuses on project planning where you're setting out the whole of the project in the list and diagrams. However, you can use the same techniques for more detailed planning at stage level and, if you need it, at a lower level still for very detailed team or work pack plans. Chapter 8 has more on working with these different levels of plan when you need them in larger projects, and also discusses when you produce the different plans.

The levels of plan bring in huge power. In a ten-stage project with up to 30 products in each phase, you'll have capacity for 300 products even before you go down to work assignment level; that's an awful lot of products, considerably more than you're likely to want on your projects.

Some conflict exists over the use of the term *Work Breakdown Structure*. In activity-led planning approaches, a Work Breakdown Structure is a diagram showing the decomposition of activities, where high-level activities are broken down into lower level activities. However, project guidance from the American space agency NASA shows the Work Breakdown Structure as products, with the very last level being the activities needed to build the products. NASA's approach is excellent, and it comes up again later in the activity planning in Chapter 6.

Unleashing WFD Power

The Work Flow Diagram (WFD) is extraordinarily useful and powerful. A big advantage of using the diagram is finding missing products. The diagram is great for this and reveals missing parts of the project that other techniques such as the Gantt Chart and activity network just don't, or don't do very well. Now that's significant because if you establish the real scope of the project at the beginning, you can then think what activities are needed to build the products and so have a more complete Project Plan. Some projects fly off the plan almost as soon as they start, and the problem isn't with the project, it's with the incomplete plan that significantly understates the project.

In a large project in a multinational company, the Project Manager decided not to use the product-planning approach and went straight in with activities and the Gantt Chart. At a progress meeting one month into the project, the project team had already discovered a lot of additional but essential work and they estimated that that after one month the project was already one month behind!

Using the WFD for risk

Your organisation is probably unique in that you have absolutely no problems with external supply. Suppliers – other organisations and other projects – always provide you with exactly what you need, exactly when you need it; they never, ever let you down. No? Oh, so you live in the real world as well then!

The Work Flow Diagram is superb for revealing dependencies on things that are coming in from outside the project. Simply look for the ovals and you see products crossing the project boundary. For each one, you can ask yourself whether the supply is likely to be a problem. In some cases, if that supply fails, you can quickly and easily get an identical or similar product from somewhere else. In other cases, though, you find that you can't easily replace the supply, and so that external dependency needs to be risk managed.

A second use of the diagram in risk management is to use it as part of the risk analysis. You can work systematically through the diagram and ask, for each product, 'What can go wrong with developing this one?' It flushes out risks that other risk analysis techniques may not find.

Using the WFD for control

Another powerful use of the Work Flow Diagram is to bring a highly effective control point into the project by deliberately creating a bottleneck. In the UK, Inspirandum used this when providing project consultancy to a power company. The company had a project to bring a new and novel approach in to control part of the operational side of power supply, but the project team members weren't sure that what they were trying to do was even theoretically possible. What they needed was a *proof of concept* product fairly early in the project. Only if they could demonstrate that the idea was at least theoretically possible would the Project Manager allow more substantial work on the project to go ahead. Dependencies were changed to make the product a bottleneck in the Work Flow Diagram.

You can get the idea of the bottleneck from the diagram in Figure 5-4. The product dependency lines originally flowed around the proof of concept product, but they were deliberately changed to create this powerful control bottleneck. Only when the proof of concept product was accepted and demonstrated that the idea was workable would authority be given to start on generating further products. And yes, if you're already thinking about delivery stage boundaries (Chapter 2 has more on stages), this product makes an ideal one because it's a major decision and commitment point in the project.

Using the WFD to show stages

The Work Flow Diagram is sequential, and because of that you can map phase or stage boundaries on it. If you wish, you can mark them on with dotted lines and so see them clearly.

Using the WFD for progress reporting

Many, or actually most, project planning tools and books suggest that you monitor progress using 'percentage complete' on activities. So, this particular activity is '60 per cent complete'. Computer planning software often shows the percentage complete on Gantt Charts by filling up the activity bar like a thermometer. Very pretty, but known to be generally unreliable. Who says the activity is 60 per cent complete; can you prove it? No, normally it's somebody's guess – sorry, somebody's estimate.

In his book *A Guide to the Successful Management of Computer Projects* (Associated Business Press), Hamish Donaldson came up with a highly amusing but very real rule that he calls the *90 per cent rule*. Hamish's rule is simply that the first 90 per cent of the activity takes 90 per cent of the time, and the last 10 per cent of the activity also takes 90 per cent of the time! It's that last little bit that goes out, and out, and out. The work is 'nearly finished', and a month later it's still 'nearly finished'.

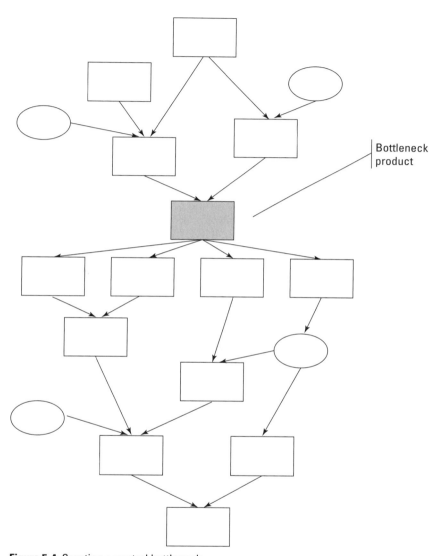

Bottleneck product

Figure 5-4: Creating a control bottleneck.

When they're saying that their task is nearly finished, perhaps the team really think it is. Then they find a huge problem and they have to do a lot of the work all over again. Or perhaps, though not in your organisation, of course, the team say 'nearly finished' to keep the Project Manager happy and off their backs for another week or two!

The thing about products is that they're either delivered or not delivered. *Delivered*, by the way, means checked and signed off. If the product hasn't been checked and signed off, then it isn't delivered. Progress monitoring, then, becomes a matter of factual reporting: which products are complete and which aren't.

You can make a useful Delivery Checklist listing all the products in a stage as milestones and, after you complete the activity planning, recording the target completion date for each product. Then, when the product is signed off, you can record the actual completion date.

Taking the progress monitoring a bit further, you can also colour code the project or stage Work Flow Diagram as suggested by Philipp Straehl, a senior Project Manager and co-developer of the PRIME method. Look at Figure 5-5 and ask yourself where the project is at this point in time.

No brainer, isn't it? Using colour or shading turns the Work Flow Diagram into a superb visual progress chart based not on an opinion or estimate of progress, but on factual reporting of delivery. You can make the diagram even more meaningful by using colours such as grey for products not yet started, orange for those underway, green for those that are finished and red for those that are overdue or which are projected to be late.

Getting a picture of the project

If you've been involved in project management for a while, think about the Gantt Chart from the project before the one you're currently working on. Can you remember it? Can you remember the one from the project before that? Can you even remember the Gantt Chart from your current project? Your answer to all three questions is likely to be 'no'. Gantt Charts are excellent, but they all look pretty much the same. A further advantage of the Work Flow Diagram is that it provides a picture of your project that's memorable and that you can hold in your head.

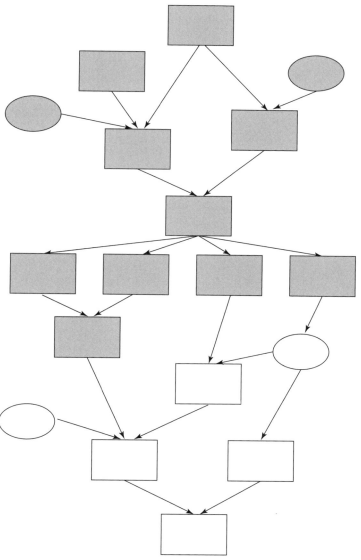

Figure 5-5: The Work Flow Diagram as a visual progress chart.

Chapter 6

You Want This Project Done When?

*P*roject assignments often have deadlines, but even if you don't have a deadline imposed on you, you'll want to know when the job will be finished. For one thing, you have other work to move on to, but then other people may need to know when your project will deliver in order to fit in with what you're delivering or changing.

When you find out the required end date, your immediate reaction is often one of panic: 'But I don't have enough time!' Don't worry, one major reason to do the planning is to make sure that you can meet the end date with time to spare.

In Chapter 5 the planning started with *products*: what it is you're going to build and deliver. But products don't have durations – a wooden table doesn't have a time span; rather, it's the activities to build the table that have the time span. To calculate the length of the project and to know what work is to be done, activity planning isn't only extremely helpful, it's essential.

The first part of activity planning is to build an Activity network. Some people think this first step is very difficult, so much so that project management software tools usually have an option to avoid the network and instead model the activity dependencies with arrows on the Gantt Chart. You don't need to miss out on the power of the activity network technique, though. Switch off the Gantt arrows option if you're using a computer tool, and prepare for something that's powerful and basically very easy. In this chapter you find out how to move from products to activities, and how to draw up an activity network that you can use to work out how long the project will take and that you can work with to help meet any fixed end date. Then, finally, you see how to move all the information onto a Gantt Chart.

Moving to Activities

Having established what the deliverables or products of the project are (Chapter 5 guides you through this work), moving to activity planning is very easy. You simply ask, 'What work is needed to build this product?' Bear in mind that you personally may not know. Don't worry, just go and ask people who do know. You can ask team members, specialists, suppliers – in fact, anyone who knows the answer. You probably already have a good idea about who to ask because you consulted them when listing and defining the products in the first place.

Having multiple tasks

There may be a single activity or task to build a particular product, but for many products you can expect to have more than one task. A simple example is with the two tasks of 'Build it' and 'Test it'. These are two tasks for a single product, often using different staff resources.

Listing the activities or tasks

You can produce a list in one of three ways: as a simple list, noting the tasks on the Work Flow Diagram or by noting the tasks on the Work Breakdown Structure (also see Chapter 5).

Here's an activity list for three products in a project to revise a company's accounts procedure. The product name forms the heading, and the indents list the activities.

Problems and requirements list

Analyse existing procedure
Interview staff
Prioritise problems and requirements list

Draft of new procedure

Draft the new procedure
Circulate the draft

Staff comments

[Await comments]

The third product, Staff comments, is an external product coming from people outside the project. By definition, then, there is no project work to be done. However, staff aren't going to send in comments in one-thousandth of a second, so a time allowance is needed in the activity plan.

Instead of writing a list, you can just add the tasks onto the Work Breakdown Structure (see Figure 6-1).

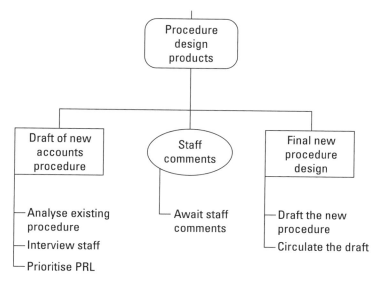

Figure 6-1: Tasks as a bottom level on the Work Breakdown Structure.

Then again, if you used a Mind Map (see Chapter 5) to add structure when thinking through the list, you can now extend this with further branches, perhaps in a different colour, to show the activities to build each of the products, around the outer edge of the Mind Map. It really doesn't really matter which approach you use as long as you end up with a list of tasks needed to build the products.

Drawing Up an Activity Network

To determine the amount of time you need for any project, you have to decide the *sequence* in which the activities will be done and how long each will take; the *duration*.

For example, suppose you have a project consisting of ten activities, each of which takes one week to complete. How long will it take you to complete your project? The truth is, you can't tell. It will take between one and ten weeks depending on how many activities you can run in parallel.

The technique that's really helpful here is the *Activity network*. Although finally the diagram will deal with project timing, you start by focusing on the sequence – the dependencies between the activities.

Computer tools are a particular help with Activity networks, and Chapter 16 has more about the software that's available. Even if you're intending to use a tool, though, it's important to understand the technique so that you properly understand what the computer tool is doing for you.

Building a Network

The Activity network Diagram isn't at all difficult to understand, so, as your starter for ten points, what do you think the diagram in Figure 6-2 means? The project has just two activities so far, A and B.

Figure 6-2: Basic activity dependency.

If you think A must be done before B, you score the ten points; well done. An equally acceptable answer is that B comes after A, so ten points for that too. Difficult, isn't it? Okay, because you're so good, here's another. Figure 6-3 shows a third activity, C, added to the project. So what can you say about when this activity is done?

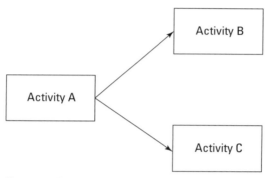

Figure 6-3: Double dependency.

Hopefully, you see that C will be done after A, or again that A must be completed before C can be started. On, then, to the really tough stuff with the addition of a final activity, D, to the project in Figure 6-4.

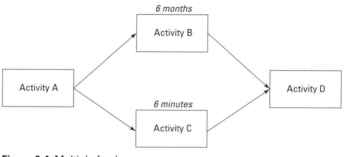

Figure 6-4: Multiple feed.

Figure 6-4 shows that you need to complete both B and C before you can start work on D.

So that's it, the diagram that people find so difficult. Really, as you've seen, it's very easy and is just a network diagram showing the tasks and the dependencies between them. You can, and will, go on to put some timings onto the activities and work out things like the project duration, but you have the main part of the technique clear already.

Before getting into the full detail of timings, try one more question on the examples with the letters. In Figure 6-4 you'll see a time duration above the boxes for Activity B and Activity C. For ten more points, what do you think the time span is between the end of Activity A and the beginning of Activity D? Look back at the diagram before you read on.

Getting the right answer to the question requires you to bear in mind that both B and C must be completed before D can start, so the time duration is six months between the end of A and the beginning of D. There seems to be quite a lot of slack time for Activity C, so it's a good one for you to do personally and have an easy time of unless, of course, C is dangerous.

If the task is dangerous you must delegate it to some junior member of the project team who's expendable. Self preservation is a vital project management principle. Clearly, it's very important that you stay alive to maximise your investment in *Project Management For Dummies*.

Using the Work Flow Diagram

The Work Flow Diagram (see Chapter 5) is a great help when moving on to the Activity network. If you take the Work Flow Diagram and lie it on its side, you have the basic framework of the Activity network already.

For a particular product, you may now have two or three activities, so you may have two or three activity boxes where you used to have one product box. You need to think through and then draw in any dependencies between those tasks.

You lie the Work Flow Diagram on its side because, by convention, Work Flow Diagrams go from top to bottom whereas Activity networks go from left to right. Although the orientation of the diagram may be mere convention and seems unimportant, if you're ever going to have to work with other people who use to these diagrams, it's best to get used to the standard approach. Reading a diagram that's flowing in a different direction from the one you're used to is surprisingly hard.

Where the dependency lines used to flow between the 'outer' product boxes, you're now attaching them to the 'inner' activity boxes. The link from a previous product may not always be to the first activity within a succeeding product box, so think carefully. Figure 6-5 provides an example in which a flow from 'Test and adjust system' feeds into 'Produce training materials' and not into the activity 'Design training materials'. That dependency is because in this project the design doesn't need screen shots from the adjusted system, but the finished materials do.

Figure 6-5 uses the procedure change project example from Chapter 5, but only part of it to keep the diagrams to a manageable size for the book. You can see that tasks have been identified for each product and the activity dependencies worked out. Although the dependencies are more detailed than those on the Work Flow Diagram (there are more boxes to deal with), the underlying dashed boxes of the products show that the framework of these dependencies was already there.

Activity planning is much faster to do if you've done product planning first. You or team specialists can more easily determine what activities are needed and estimate how long they are likely to take, rather than just guessing.

Putting in the time durations

Now comes the bit where this technique starts to reveal some real power. Having established the dependencies between activities (see the previous section), the next step is to put some times onto the activities and, among other things, work out how long the project is going to take. For each activity, you need an estimate of how long it will take to do it.

Understanding staff hours and elapsed time

The Activity network works with calendar time, sometimes referred to as *elapsed time*. If you have a task to do that requires ten days' effort, but you can only spare half of each day to work on it, it's going to take you 20 elapsed days. Equally, if you can work on it full time and a colleague can work with you and can also devote full days, then that ten days of staff effort will only take five days of elapsed time – provided you don't get distracted and start arguing about the football or pop idols.

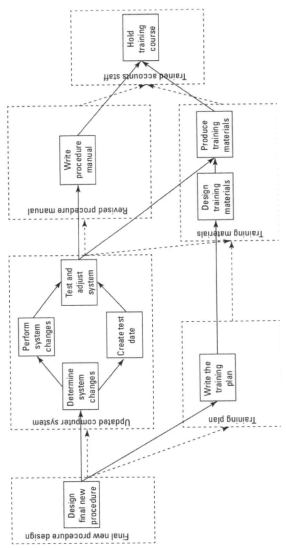

Figure 6-5: The Activity network based on the Work Flow Diagram.

At first, you can put in a provisional duration based on the amount of staff resource you expect to be available. You can make adjustments later; these are the initial timings.

Estimating – the tricky bit

There's no way out of it – estimating is difficult to get right. If you find a way of getting accurate estimates every time, then patent the idea quickly and prepare to be very rich.

Different industries have different approaches to estimating, but the bottom line is that the most useful information you can have to hand is how long it took last time you did an activity like this. It's worth keeping historic information from past projects because they can be an invaluable source of estimating data for future projects. Where you don't have that information, you do the best you can, but remember you can always ask other people too, such as technical specialists in the organisation. This is where product planning comes in useful, because you can say exactly what it is you're building, and in turn that helps the specialists estimate more accurately based on their experience.

You'll find more detail on estimating in the section 'Estimating Activity Durations', towards the end of the chapter, but if you're new to Activity networks, then stay focused on the technique itself for the moment.

Thinking a bit more about duration

The following can all affect an activity's duration:

- ✔ The amount of work effort required to complete the activity
- ✔ People's availability
- ✔ Whether people can work on the activity at the same time
- ✔ Availability and capacity of non-staff resources (for example, a computer's processing speed)
- ✔ Delay (for example, if your boss takes a couple of days to get around to spending an hour reading your proposal)

In many cases, you can see up front that the duration of an activity is dependent on something other than work effort. This situation is quite common in business projects where a manager who's both very senior and very busy must do something. That manager may tell you that she'll do the three days' project work you need from her, but she can't tell you exactly when she'll do it within a given two-week period because her availability depends on the other demands on her time. In that case, you can enter the activity into the plan as 'fixed duration' of two weeks, and note separately for project costing that in fact it involves only three days of that manager's time.

Understanding the basis of a duration estimate also helps you work out ways to reduce it. For example, suppose you estimate a test requires 24 hours running on a specialised machine. If you can use the machine for only six hours a day, the test duration is four days. Doubling the number of people working on the test won't reduce the duration to two days, but getting approval to use the machine for 12 hours a day, perhaps at night, will.

Calculating the length of the project

The next bit is very easy, provided that you've mastered basic addition and subtraction, like 2 + 3 = 5. So, assuming that you're aged 6 or over, this step in building the Activity network shouldn't present too much of a problem. (If you're under 6, then you're getting a real jump start in your project management career.)

In Figure 6-6 you now see some smaller boxes inside the activity box – in fact, seven of them. You may think that these smaller boxes will make the diagram look busy, but in fact they make all the calculations very easy and very mechanical. The duration goes in the top-middle box and you choose your scale. The scale is normally elapsed days or you can use weeks; the examples that follow use weeks.

0	3	3
	Activity A	

Figure 6-6: Calculating the earliest finish date.

In Figure 6-6 you can see that the top-left box has been set to zero, which is the beginning of the project and which is the earliest start date for that first activity. The top-right box is the earliest finish date. So, the activity starts at zero and is three weeks long. So when is the earliest the activity can finish? Here's the formula you need:

Earliest start date + duration = earliest finish date

0 + 3 = 3, so the answer is the end of Week 3. Tricky, huh?

You can use calendar dates rather than day or week numbers. You'll find more about working with calendar dates in the nearby sidebar named, with normal *Dummies* guide precision, 'Working with calendar dates'.

Now, you know from the dependency arrow that the next activity can start the moment that the first activity finishes: in the example, the end of Week 3. You may think that sounds a little weird and it should be the beginning of Week 4, but stay with 'end of week' for the moment because it makes the calculation very easy and very mechanical. So, just copy the figure from the top-right box of the first activity into the top-left box of any other activity coming after it and directly connected with an arrow.

Stick to the arrow pathways at all times. Take care not to jump across the network to an activity that isn't directly connected by an arrow, or it will all go horribly wrong.

You can see the whole Activity network calculated forwards in Figure 6-7.

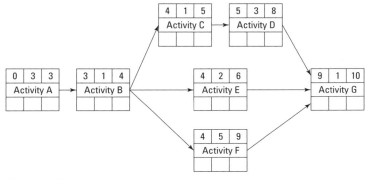

Figure 6-7: The forward pass to find the project duration.

The earliest start date of an activity is the same as the earliest finish date from the activity directly in front of it. Figure 6-7 reveals a bit of a problem with the last activity in the project, because three activities feed into it, not just one. In the case of more than one activity feeding in, take the highest figure or, if you're working with calendar dates, the latest date. Flick back to Figure 6-5 where the time gap across the middle of that simple network was six months, not six minutes. The point is that all the preceding activities must be finished before the current one can start, so it's the highest number from all the feeder activities that determines the start point of this one.

The Activity network now starts to earn its keep because you can see that this project will take ten weeks. The total of the activity durations is 16 weeks, but the project will complete in less time because some activities can be done in parallel.

Working with calendar dates

An option with the Activity network is to work with calendar dates rather than day or week numbers. That's fine, and all the computer tools do that. In one way it makes the network easier to understand, but in another way it's more difficult, so don't expect to find a perfect approach. If you're using a computer tool to plan the project, which is sensible if the project is anything more than very small, just one of the problems you encounter is with the start date.

Imagine you want to plan the project out but you haven't got approval for it yet, so you don't know exactly when it will start. You go to your computer tool, and as soon as you've got the project name in, it starts demanding to know the day on which you'll start the project. You don't know, but you find to your annoyance that the tool won't move off that screen until you've entered a start date. In frustration, you enter '1 November', which is in two weeks' time. As you then put in durations, the tool tells you that you can't schedule work for certain days because they're end-of-year public holidays and aren't working days. 'But,' you explain patiently to the screen, 'those activities may not clash with holidays because I may not get approval for this project until January anyway.' Then you look more closely at your computer and realise it doesn't have ears.

Nick saw a great cartoon of a bear sitting in front of a PC having just smashed a huge paw through the screen. The caption was, 'Please enter your response'. Computer tools for project scheduling are great but they can be really frustrating sometimes and make you want to emulate the bear.

Understanding Float

It's useful to know which activities have some slack time, and that's the next thing to find out. This is a great help when managing the project, because if someone reports that her activity is more difficult than she thought and will take a week longer than planned, you know immediately whether you can absorb that week or whether it may cause a problem. Going back to the example of doing a six-minute activity in parallel with a six-month one (see the earlier section 'Seeing how you build up an Activity network'), you aren't going to lose a lot of sleep if the six-minute activity ends up taking ten minutes, because you still have a vast amount of time to spare.

The term *slack* is a very descriptive one for the amount of spare time for an activity. However, the international word for this time is *float* and computer tools usually use that term.

The first step in working out the float is to copy down the earliest finish date of the last activity – as shown in the top-right box – into the box at the bottom right, which is the latest finish date. In the example in Figure 6-7, the time shown for Activity G is ten weeks. Then you work back on the bottom line, going from right to left. What you want to calculate and put in the bottom-left box is the latest start date for that activity.

So, if the activity must finish at the end of Week 10 and is one week long, when is the latest you could start it without going beyond the ten weeks? Given that the activity will take one week to complete, if you start any later than the end of Week 9, you won't be finished by the end of Week 10. Remember, you're working with 'end of week' figures here. To calculate the latest start, you simply subtract the activity duration from the latest finish date:

Latest finish date – duration = latest start date

So, the mind-boggling calculation is 10 – 1 = 9; the latest start date is the end of Week 9. Now copy that latest start date into the bottom-right box of any activity directly connected to this one by an arrow, to provide its latest finish date; follow the arrows backwards. As before, take care to follow only the arrow pathways, and whatever you do, don't jump across the network where no direct arrow connection exists. Figure 6-8 shows the result.

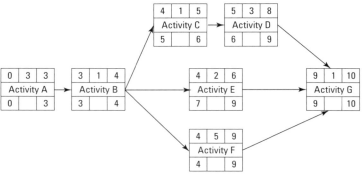

Figure 6-8: The backwards pass.

Activity B is tricky because three activities feed back into it, so which of the three different figures is the right one? The answer on the backwards pass return trip is to take the lowest figure or, if you're using calendar dates, the earliest date. In Figure 6-8 the three options for Activity B were 5, 7 and 4, so the correct figure is 4.

If you've done all the mathematics correctly and stuck carefully to the arrow pathways, you should end up back on the far left-hand side of the diagram with zero as the latest start date of the first activity. In Figure 6-8 it is; whew!

Now, this is where the diagram gets more interesting and even more powerful. It shows, for example, that people can start working on Activity F at the end of Week 4. But the network also shows that the start of Activity F can be postponed right up to the end of Week 7 without causing a problem, because the end of Week 7 is the latest start date. That's three weeks of spare time. You can work out the float on each of the activities, and that goes in the middle box on the bottom line.

You can calculate float in different ways, but the safest one is to compare the figures in the two right-hand boxes for each activity: the earliest finish date and the latest finish date. Here's the formula:

Latest finish date − earliest finish date = float

The next figure, Figure 6-9, shows the result.

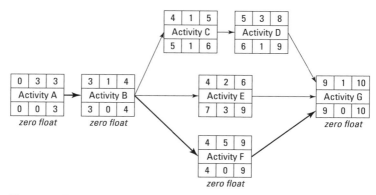

Figure 6-9: The completed Activity network.

Knowing the float is actually a bit better than just knowing whether you can delay the start of an activity, as you may have already realised. The float tells you how much spare time you have for that activity, whether it's in postponing the start date or the activity taking a bit longer than estimated.

Identifying the Critical Path

You may have heard of Critical Path Analysis (CPA) — or Critical Path Method (CPM) – and think it sounds daunting. However, the good news is that Critical Path Analysis is very easy; in fact, if you've made an activity network (see the previous sections), then you've done most of the work already.

The *critical path* is simply the longest chain of dependent activities going through the activity network. You can see it clearly, because critical path activities all have a float of zero (the previous section explains float). Figure 6-9 shows this path with the heavy arrows. The critical path is significant because, as the longest path, it determines the duration of the project. The durations of the activities along the heavy lines in Figure 6-9 total ten weeks, the length of the project.

The critical path is important in managing the project, because if you get a delay on a critical path activity, the longest path gets longer. If the longest path gets longer, that means that the project end date goes out. So slippage on a critical path activity doesn't just affect that activity but the entire project.

As you manage the project, monitor all the activities carefully, but especially look out for the critical path. You also have to consider the resource – Chapters 7 has more on that.

Watching the critical path

Planning isn't just something you do at the start of a project, but rather something you do continuously right the way through. Things change, and unless yours is the first, no project ever goes *exactly* to plan. Strangely, that's what makes the plan even more important: it's something you adjust in order to keep the project on track.

Staying with the example of the network used in Figures 6-7 to 6-9, imagine there's a problem part way through the project as Activity C is being done. The team leader reports two delays: one because a supplier was late delivering something needed for C, and one because half the team have suddenly become ill and have gone home. The team leader tells you that Activity C is now going to take three weeks instead of the planned one week and she can do absolutely nothing to pull the time back. So what's the impact on the project of this two-week delay?

Your first reaction may be that there is no overall impact, because there is a week of float on C and also on the following activity, D, so these will offset the two-week delay. However, if you look at the calculations on the top of the boxes in Figure 6-10, you'll find they tell a rather different story, and the project has been extended by one week.

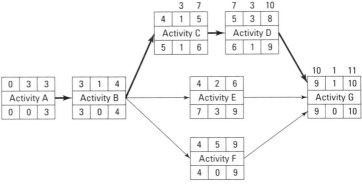

Figure 6-10: A changing critical path.

Two types of float

The Project Management Institute (PMI) identifies two types of float:

- **Total float:** The total amount of time by which a scheduled activity may be delayed without delaying the project end date or a schedule constraint. So in Figure 6-10, Activity C has a week of total float because it can be delayed for that long without affecting the overall project. That

is the float that you enter in the bottom-middle box.

- **Free float:** The amount of time by which a scheduled activity may be delayed without delaying the early start of any immediately following scheduled activities. In the case of Activity C, that would be zero. Any delay at all on C would affect the start of the following Activity D.

The reason for the project delay is that Activities C and D are in an uninterrupted chain (no dependency arrows between C and D going out to other activities or coming in) and the one-week float on each of these two activities is actually the same week. So, of the two-week delay, one week has been absorbed by the float and the other week has pushed the project out by a week. Because of this change in C and D, that chain has now become the longest one in that part of the project, so the critical path moves as shown by the heavy arrows in Figure 6-10. If you recalculate the diagram on the backwards pass (see the section 'Understanding float'), you find that Activity F, which used to be on the critical path, now has a week of float.

Be careful if, on your project's Activity network Diagram, you have, for example, an uninterrupted chain of three activities each showing five days' float (the float figure will always be the same on each activity in an uninterrupted chain). Along that chain you have five days' float, not 15. This is known as *dependent float*. If you use all or part of the float in one activity, you've lost that much on the remaining activities in that chain.

Finding a split critical path

For good measure, here's one final twist. Suppose the team leader doing the work on Activity C comes to see you again, but this time with some good news. There's still a problem with the supplier, but the sick team members are now all back at work having had a 24-hour stomach upset after a dodgy takeaway (carryout, if you're a Scot) lunch. The team leader tells you that there is still a delay on C, but it will now only be a one-week delay, not a two-week delay. The activity will now take two weeks instead of the original planned one week.

The one-week delay is now completely taken up by the float, and the project reverts to ten weeks, but now both the top and bottom branches of the network are the same length, so the critical path splits into two for this part of the project. You normally have a single path. But if the critical path does split into two or even more for a while, don't worry – it can happen, and in the example it just did.

Being Precise with Dependencies

The activity network you create with the help of the previous sections provides some great information. But you can enhance the diagram notation to give you even greater precision with the dependencies.

Knowing the dependency types

The examples in all the activity networks so far in this chapter have needed a dependency where an activity cannot start until work on the previous one(s) has been completed, the most common dependency type.

Finish to start

So, the most common sort. When you have finished one activity, you can start the succeeding one(s). It's good to know that project management isn't bound up in jargon, and this type of dependency is known as a *finish to start*.

The overlap, or lead

This is in which you don't have to wait for the first activity to be completely finished before you start the next one. Figure 6-11 shows the notation.

Figure 6-11: The overlap.

Think of a project to write and test computer programs. You don't usually have to wait until all the programs are written before you can start testing. As soon as a set of programs are finished, you can start testing them while programmers are still writing other programs. It's important that you spot overlaps, so you don't build unnecessary delay into your plan.

The start to start

A *start to start* dependency is like the ultimate overlap. You can't start Activity B before Activity A, but as soon as you've got going with A, you can begin B. That means that the earliest start date of Activity B will be the same as the earliest start date of A. Have a look at Figure 6-12.

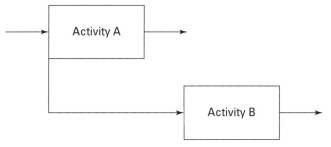

Figure 6-12: The start to start.

In a 250-kilometre gas pipeline project, a trench was dug for the pipe, but optical fibre was also put in the trench to carry control signals such as those needed to operate the valves. The optical fibre couldn't be put in first, because laying the gas pipe would have damaged it, but as soon as the first length of pipe was in, the optical fibre could be put in on top.

The lag

Sometimes there is a delay after an activity before a second one can start. You can show this in two ways.

First, you can put in a dummy activity of 'waiting time', which can be good because it makes the waiting time visible rather than having a weird gap in the project when you come to look at the Gantt Chart. In the example in the section 'Listing the activities or tasks', earlier in this chapter, the dummy activity is in square brackets so it can be seen at a glance that it doesn't involve project work.

The second way to show a delay after an activity before a second one can start is to put a lag time on the dependency line. You need to adjust the earliest start date of the following activity if there is a lag. If Activity A can finish at the end of Week 6, then Activity B doesn't begin at the end of Week 6 but rather at the end of Week 10 if you have a four-week lag, as with the example in Figure 6-13.

Figure 6-13: The lag.

An example is with sending out contracts to newly recruited staff and holding the induction training. Unless you're recruiting people who are currently unemployed, you're likely to have to wait four weeks before they arrive, because they need to work a period of notice with their current employers.

The finish to finish

The final dependency example is the finish to finish. You may be able to start Activity B early on, but you can't finish it until Activity A is finished. Figure 6-14 shows this finish-to-finish notation.

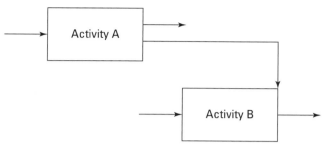

Figure 6-14: The finish to finish.

Consider a project to produce a four-page company brochure. Activity A is to write the text and Activity B is to design the brochure. Now, because the text is important stuff, the managing director wants to write it herself. You do a lot on the design, but you can't finish it with that last tweak to the layout until you know exactly what the final text is.

The finish to finish affects your calculations because the end of Activity B will be determined by the end of Activity A, not the addition of the earliest start date of B to its duration.

Using computers

Having hit out a bit at computers in the sidebar 'Working with calendar dates', earlier in the chapter, it's time to redress the balance and praise them up a bit. When you have anything more than a small activity network, and when you start to use the more sophisticated dependencies, the computer tools come to the fore despite their limitations. They perform in a blink of an eye calculations that would have you scratching your head for quite some time – just make sure that you've entered the dependencies and timings absolutely correctly.

Chapter 16 has much more on using computer software in projects, and to whet your appetite you can get some of it for free.

Staying in touch with reality

There is a danger that you can get very focused on your network and become so absorbed in the times and dependency arrows that you lose touch with reality. If funding for an activity won't be available until the start of the new financial year, then that's the activities start point and not the end of the previous activity which may be much earlier.

If you're using a computer tool, you can deal with this situation quite easily by specifying a fixed start date for an activity – in this case first day of the financial year. Make a note in the plan to remind yourself both that you've anchored the start date (in case circumstances change) and the reason, which in this case is the availability of finance. Other reasons include interaction with other projects where staff won't be available to work on your project until they've finished work on another that's higher priority. Please see Chapter 7 for more on resourcing.

Thinking more about sequences

In thinking through the dependencies for your network, you will find that some things are fixed but others are a matter of choice:

- **Mandatory dependencies:** These relationships must be observed if project work is to be a success. They include:

  - **Hard logic:** Certain processes must logically occur before others. For example, when building a house, you must build the foundations before the frame.

  - **Legal requirements:** Some laws or regulations require that certain activities be done before others. For example, a drug must go through clinical trials before it is mass produced for distribution.

  - **Procedural requirements:** Company policies and procedures require that certain activities be done before others. Audit must approve your design for the new financial system before you start to build it.

✔ **Discretionary dependencies:** You may choose to establish these relationships between activities, but they
aren't required. They include:

- **Choices:** You have to perform Activities C, D and E.
Your work will be too fragmented if you work on all
three at the same time so you choose to work on
Activity D first, then E and then C, perhaps getting
the most difficult one out of the way first.

- **Logical dependencies:** Performing certain activities
before others sometimes seems to make the most
sense. Because so much of Chapters 1 and 2 in your
report depend on what you write in Chapter 3, you
decide to write Chapter 3 first.

✔ **External dependencies:** Starting a project activity may
require that an activity outside the project be completed.
For example, you can't start a particular test activity until
your organisation's test laboratory receives and installs a
new piece of test equipment that's currently on order.

Discriminate very clearly between activity dependencies that
are mandatory and those that you've chosen, and note the
details in your plan. Where you've chosen to do things in a
particular sequence, you can alter it later if you change your
mind. You can't change your mind about the legal constraints
affecting activity sequence, though; they're fixed and you
must live with them. Notes in the plan also help other people
to understand why you've set up the dependencies in a particular way.

To give a more meaningful example than A's, B's and C's,
Figure 6-15 is the activity network for part of the business
change project example from the earlier chapters.

The example in Figure 6-15 is still a 'first cut' and now needs
to be examined to see, for example, whether some of the relationships are something other than finish to start.

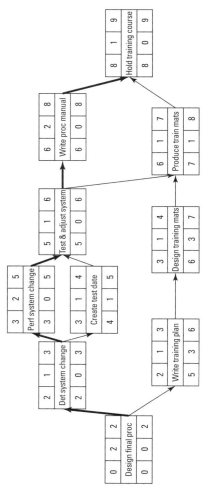

Figure 6-15: Activity network (Precedence Network type) for the example project.

Working with the Network

With the network you build up through the guidance of the previous sections, it's still early days with the activity planning but the network already reveals useful information. Even before you finish the network, you can see whether you can meet any required end date. You can also get useful preliminary information from the critical path.

In the project example in Figure 6-14 in the section 'Being Precise with Dependencies', it's clear that computer work is going to determine the length of the project. You may already be making a mental note, then, to make doubly sure that the computer people have the time put aside for this job so that it won't get delayed. Such thinking is actually a start into risk management (see Chapter 9). A lot of risks come to light during planning; note them down and start thinking about them now.

Something else you may notice from the network, if you already know who'll be doing what, is a resource constraint. If you happen to know that the person who's making the adjustments to the computer system is the same person who'll be producing the test data, then although these two activities aren't dependent on each other logically, a resource dependency exists because one person can't do two full-time jobs simultaneously. That resource conflict foreshadows the resource planning of Chapter 7.

You may be starting to think that this planning stuff is really interesting, but it's also getting rather detailed. The answer to both issues is, 'Yes, it is, isn't it?' The detail is important, however, because it recognises the reality of the project. Taking the example of the resource conflict for the person adjusting the computer system, it's just not possible to do two full-time jobs on the project simultaneously. The resource issue is a genuine project-planning problem that needs to be resolved; it's not merely a matter of fine detail that's over the top and not really necessary.

Working to meet end dates

If your network shows you can't meet a required date, don't panic. With the product and activity plans, you have powerful tools you can work with to adjust the project so that it will fit – and with time to spare for contingency.

Inspirandum project management courses are fun as well as hard work. Nick often teases groups when their case study plans (often for one of the organisation's live projects) fail to meet the required end date. He talks in low 'gloom and doom'

tones and asks whether the plan has failed. The group members invariably say that it has, to which he responds that, on the contrary, the plan is already a huge success. Even before finishing the activity network, the group hasn't only discovered that at present the project won't work, but it can say exactly what the shortfall is. Now that the problem is visible and sized, the group can work on the plans to get the project in balance.

You can't finalise the plan when you've done the Activity network because there is still the whole area of resource planning to consider. You do get early warning of a timing problem, though, if your Activity network shows that you will miss the end date. There will be things that you can do, and not least to identify activities that could be shortened or *crashed* by adding extra resource (usually, but not always, extra staff). If you do find activities that can be crashed, you can try to get some extra resource for your project and take that into account when starting the resource planning.

You may well be looking to reduce the duration of a number of activities, but clearly your primary focus will be the critical path (see 'Identifying the Critical Path', earlier in this chapter). Being the longest path and the one that determines the length of the project, that's the set of activities that you must ultimately reduce in duration. That may even mean leaving some out and so reducing the scope of the project to fit the time available.

Backing into the schedule

When working with the schedule, it can be tempting to try and make the activities fit the time available (backing into the schedule) instead of calculating the time needed to do those activities. Don't do it! If you reduce the estimates to fit, you simply end up with an unrealistic plan and a late or even failed project.

In the States, Stan Portny was reviewing a colleague's Project Plan a while back and noticed that she had allowed one week for her final report's review and approval. When he asked her whether she thought this estimate was realistic, she replied that it certainly wasn't realistic, but that she had to use that estimate for the Project Plan to work out. In other words, she was using time estimates that totalled to the number she *wanted* to reach rather than ones she thought she *could* meet.

Going for Gantt

At last, something that's likely to be more familiar territory: the Gantt Chart with its horizontal bars showing activities against a time scale. The chart was devised by the American management consultant, Henry Gantt, getting on for 100 years ago. He is most remembered for the chart named after him that's at the hub of most project management tools today.

The Gantt Chart is powerful but, perhaps predictably, it doesn't do everything. Used in combination with an Activity network, it's extremely useful.

If you're using a computer tool, getting to the Gantt is automatic. As you draw the network, you find that you can switch view and see the same data in the form of a Gantt Chart. In line with the overall approach of this chapter, though, it helps if you see how to do it 'by hand' so that even if you do use a computer tool, you understand what it's doing.

Here's how to produce a Gantt Chart:

1. **List the activities.**

   Just copy in your activity list with the products as milestones or headings, and the activities to build each product listed under its heading.

2. **Draw the bars.**

   Take three figures from each activity box on the activity network: top left, top right and bottom right, which are the earliest start date, earliest finish date and latest finish date. These figures mark the three points on the Gantt bar with float at the back end. Critical path activities, of course, don't have float, so the earliest and latest finish are the same.

Figure 6-16 shows how the figures on the Activity network map onto the Gantt bar. Because the figure is using week numbers, the position on the Gantt bar relates to 'end of week'. If you're using calendar dates, then the bottom scale will be actual dates not just week numbers.

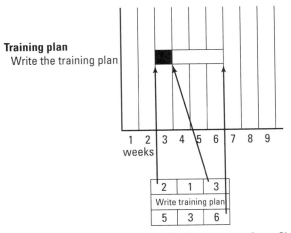

Figure 6-16: Moving from the Activity Network to a Gantt Chart.

To give a more complete example, Figure 6-17 shows the activities for the sample project plotted onto the Gantt Chart.

Figure 6-17: The Gantt Chart for the example project.

Gantt Charts are both powerful and popular because you can easily see the project mapped out, and they provide a view of where you are. You can use the chart at more than one level of detail, and computer tools allow you to 'roll up' part or all of the chart to show less detail, such as only displaying project-plan-level activities. You can also open out the task list to work on the more detailed activities when you get into planning at a lower level for each stage.

During the project, steering committees often like to keep sight of the big picture. So it's the project level of detail that senior managers often ask for in progress reports.

Gantt Charts are excellent, but as Figure 6-17 demonstrates, they don't show everything. For example, the critical path is hard to see, but also if it moved because of a change in the duration of an activity, where would it go? You can see the pathways easily enough on an activity network, but you can't see them on the Gantt.

Estimating Activity Durations

The *estimate* isn't how long you want the activity to take or how long someone tells you it must take; the estimate is how long you think it really will take. Because estimating is quite difficult to get right, and because if the estimates are significantly out it undermines the plan, this last section of the chapter focuses on some issues to bear in mind and outlines some techniques that may help.

Unrealistically short duration estimates can lead to an interesting array of serious project problems:

- ✔ The work simply can't be done in the time set down on the plan, so the project goes wildly off track and becomes very hard to control. The plan is hopelessly unrealistic and so virtually useless as a management tool.

- ✔ Because unrealistic estimates appear to meet your schedule's targets, you don't seek realistic alternative strategies that increase the chances of accomplishing activities in required durations.

- ✔ Because the work actually takes longer than the plan allows, delivery will be late – delivery of the end product but perhaps also products that are being taken into operational use during the project. That causes disruption to the business, including dependent projects, that expected things to be in place at a certain time.

✔ If people believe duration estimates are totally unrealistic, they stop trying to achieve them. When delays occur during an activity, people accept them as inevitable instead of seeking ways to overcome them.

✔ Quality goes out of the window as team members race to throw things together to get somewhere near to the deadlines – the planned tests and checks become a joke. However, those on the receiving end of the deliverables don't share the humour when things don't work properly and cause operational problems.

✔ When your project fails to meet the end date or quality has suffered badly, both the project and you are perceived as failures.

Getting the best information

In a small project where you're familiar with the work, you can probably come up with the estimates yourself. However, after the project moves beyond small and starts to involve more skill sets and people, you almost certainly need to consult others. Where you don't know the project area at all (and that doesn't mean that you shouldn't manage the project), you'll need a lot of input from other people.

When estimating an activity's duration, consider past experience, including any records of previous projects you can get your hands on, expert opinion and other available sources of information. The more important your project and the more significant the deadline, the more you need to do to clarify the different components of the activity when estimating:

✔ **Physical processes:** Fixed durations for things, such as concrete curing and paint drying.

✔ **Time delays:** Such as waiting for supply after ordering.

✔ **Work needing physical resources:** Activities that computers and other machines perform, such as running a trial batch on the production line that goes at a set speed.

> ✔ **Work performed by people:** Physical and mental activities that people perform, such as writing a report, assembling a piece of equipment and thinking of ideas for an ad campaign.

When you look for information and advice to help with estimating, think about asking experts who are familiar with the work, records from similar tasks in past projects and staff who will be doing the work and who have an understanding of it. You can also use estimating techniques.

Delphi and Modified Delphi

Had you been an ancient Greek, you might have sought guidance from the oracle at Delphi. How the oracle actually worked is lost in the mists of time, but one theory is that it was a group of wise people who consulted between themselves and then gave a single answer. Similarly, you can ask people for estimates using the Delphi technique. As to whether they're wise or not . . .

The *Delphi technique* works well in a workshop. You explain an activity and then get everyone to write down how long they think it will take to carry out the activity. You then gather up the individual estimates, calculate the average and use that as the estimate in the plan.

Modified Delphi is where you take the estimating a step further. Having got everyone's opinion, you identify the person who gave the most optimistic estimate and the person with the most pessimistic estimate and ask them to explain their thinking. Everyone listens carefully then they estimate again. You take the average and put it in your plan.

Three-point estimating

Three-point estimating establishes the best case, worst case and most likely case. Although you will almost certainly use the most likely value for the plan, it may help to note the best and worst cases so other people can see the range and not get too worried if the work goes a bit beyond the estimate, in either direction, during the project.

Giving a health warning

You won't find an easy way of getting estimates right, but you can do three things about the inherent uncertainty:

✓ **Allow additional contingency.** The more uncertain you are about the estimates, the more time you need to allow for things taking longer than anticipated.

✓ **Warn people.** Note in the plan that the estimates may be incorrect. You can state your confidence in the estimates, such as that in one part of the project you're 90 per cent confident that the estimates are close.

✓ **Update the estimates and the plan.** When better information comes to hand as the project continues, feed that new information into the plan.

Chapter 7

Looking at Resources

Stan Portny remembers reading the following from a stressed-out Project Manager: 'We've done so much with so little for so long, they now expect us to do everything with nothing!'

The truth is, of course, you can't accomplish anything with nothing, and in the context of project resource planning, you need people, money and often equipment and facilities. Many Project Managers tend to underestimate this resourcing – don't be daunted by it, but instead allow time to think it through and plan thoroughly. That means getting the best out of your staff – almost certainly the most important factor – but also equipment and funding. By the way, using project staff well isn't selfish either. Good project management includes giving team members opportunities to succeed and develop alongside you getting a successful project, and that needs careful thought and planning too.

This chapter covers resource planning. It helps you understand the dynamics of scheduling and includes areas such as availability to show that full-time staff aren't really full time. On the staffing side, the chapter also covers topics such as individual performance, multi-tasking and the working environment, all of which can have a big impact on your Project Plan. The chapter then deals with physical resources such as equipment and financial resource.

Seeing the Need for Plans

Before you roll your sleeves up and get stuck in to the detail of how to plan your use of staff and physical (non-staff) resource on the project, it's helpful to be clear about *why* you need to do this planning.

Dealing with resource conflicts

The first reason that you need to plan staff resource is that your use of staff can conflict in several ways with something else. Resource conflicts make your plan completely unworkable if you don't deal with them.

Here are three examples of resource conflict:

- ✔ **Multiple tasks:** The plan has a number of activities including three which will take a month each. The activity network shows that the three can be done in parallel and each one involves Sue working full time. However, unless Sue is Superwoman and can work three shifts a day of eight hours each – 24-hour working – for a whole month, we seem to have a problem.

- ✔ **Calendar events:** A task is three days' duration and Sue is required to work eight hours a day. On the plan, the task is to be done from 1 to 3 January. But now there's a problem with the calendar. Because 1 January is a public holiday, there are only two working days in that period, not three, so the task can't be achieved. The plan isn't going to work unless this is sorted out because the offices are shut on 1 January and Sue just won't be there. Oh yes, and four months ago she booked annual leave for 2 and 3 January because it's her husband's 30th birthday and she's booked a surprise trip to Paris, and although Sue appreciates that the project is quite important . . .

- ✔ **Other projects:** For another task, Sue is needed for five days for the week commencing 8 February. Oh joy, she isn't working on any other project activity during that week and neither are there any public holidays or birthday surprises. But now we find that another project also needs her for five days in the week commencing 8 February. Unfortunately, that other project has a much higher priority than ours.

The last of these conflicts reveals the messy but realistic situation that you sometimes find yourself in: sorting out resourcing between projects, not just within your own. You must allow time for planning at the front end of your project, because if you don't sort these problems out on the plan they'll hit you later on during the project when they'll be even harder to deal with. Picking up the last example again, Sue isn't going to be working on the project on 8 February even if it's on the plan in red letters, bold type and underlined. If it stays on the plan that she'll be there, the plan is unrealistic and the project will hit a major problem on 8 February.

Having, hopefully, convinced you that resource conflicts, for both staff and physical resource, can cause problems, you may now be wondering how you actually resolve them. The later section 'Smoothing the resource' will help, after a closer examination of the dynamics and nature of staff resourcing.

Checking availability

Another reason you need to plan staff resource is so you can tell people when you'll need them and arrange, if necessary, for their managers to release them to work on the project. The resource plan makes everything visible, and people who are taking part in the project or who are authorising the staff hours can make sure they can meet the commitment in terms of the number of staff, the particular skills and people involved, and the dates that you actually need them. That word *commitment* is significant because you don't want empty promises that cause you problems later if the resource doesn't materialise.

The same argument applies to physical resource. In some cases equipment must be borrowed or hired so you need to be sure it will be there when you need it. If there's some doubt about that availability, that may raise the question of whether it would be better to buy it rather than hire or borrow it.

Monitoring use of staff

Some organisations have procedures and even systems that detail and track every resource on every project. Other organisations don't formally plan or track project resources at all. However, even if your organisation doesn't require you to plan your resource needs and track your resource use, doing so is vital to your project's success. Even in terms of progress and control, how can you tell whether the project is on track if you don't know whether the actual use of staff hours on work so far is as you expected?

Planning the Staff Resource

Your project's success rests on your ability to get the right people to perform your project's work. That may be in terms of suitably qualified staff or simply just getting enough people – which isn't always so easy. You begin your project planning by looking at what you need to deliver (see Chapter 5 for details on how to do this). Next, you decide what activities you'll need performed to create the deliverables (see Chapter 6). Your third step is to decide what skills and knowledge people must have to perform the activities.

Working out the needs for skills and knowledge

To determine the skills and knowledge that people must have for your project, you can work from the Product Definitions produced as part of your planning (refer to Chapter 5). You now develop that thinking as you consider the staff resource needs in more detail.

You determine the skill and knowledge requirements by reviewing what is to be built, but as with planning, don't panic if you aren't sure or simply don't know. Remember that being a Project Manager doesn't usually mean that you're a technical expert, so go and talk to other people including:

- Any Project Managers who've run similar projects in the past
- Possible external supplier companies
- Staff who've worked on similar projects in the past.
- Subject matter experts
- Your project office, which may have plans and other documents showing staff resource on similar past projects

For most situations, you need to know two pieces of information about a task to determine the qualifications that a person must have to perform it:

✔ The required levels of proficiency in the needed skills and knowledge

✔ Whether the assignment entails:

- Working under someone else's guidance when applying the skills or knowledge

- Working alone to apply the skills or knowledge

- Managing others who are applying the skills or knowledge

Growing your people

As you think through the tasks you'll usually need to consider staff development. You want to progress in your career, and so too do your project staff. You need to bear in mind individual needs for development and organisational needs for increasingly skilled staff, as well getting the project delivered.

Developing skills

As you look through the project tasks, you can look for flexibility so people can work on things to learn new skills and increase competence in existing ones. In this way:

✔ You help the organisation develop its skills base.

✔ You interest and motivate staff, who are enjoying what they're doing and are challenged by it.

For example, you might allocate someone to something that's new for him but where the task has got a bit of spare time, or put him alongside someone else who's already experienced.

Using the critical path

Chapter 6 covered the critical path technique, and that comes in useful here. If a task is on the critical path, by definition there's no spare time on it; you'll therefore usually want to assign very competent and experienced people to do the work. Equally, if a task has a lot of float (slack) time, it may be more suitable for less experienced staff. If the work takes a bit longer to do it than planned, then there won't be any time impact because of the float time on the activity.

Explaining yourself to experienced staff

Having adjusted the plan to develop inexperienced staff, don't now neglect your more experienced people. More experienced staff like a challenge, and if you only allocate them to the mundane tasks that all happen to be on the critical path, they're going to get bored and demotivated. Try to make sure that experienced staff get some of the more juicy project work, and where you do need them to work on something boring because it's critical or helping to develop a more junior team member, you can at least explain why and hold out the promise of something more substantial later on.

If you're now thinking that there's a lot to bear in mind when dealing with staff resource on a project, yes, there is.

Fine Tuning Your Estimates

When drawing up the Activity Network and Gantt Chart (see Chapter 6), you already made some estimates of how long each activity will take. The estimates may be based on good information such as where you already know exactly who'll do that task and his level of experience. However, it may have been little more than a guess just to get the basic framework of the plan in place. Now's the time to work on the detail of the estimates and make sure that there are no conflicts.

If you're using a computer-based project management tool, it will almost certainly include a calendar facility, so you can avoid some of the areas of resource conflict. The software will hold details of public holidays, and will usually have an additional calendar for each person working on the project, so you can enter their availability information, including booked holidays. Good news for Sue's husband then (see the earlier section 'Dealing with resource conflicts').

Factors in activity timing

Resource scheduling is inherently complicated, so don't get worried if things start to look difficult. Just work through in a methodical way and everything will come right in the end. It's tempting to focus simply on the figures when scheduling staff resource, but other factors can have an impact. Here are a few things to bear in mind as you work through the estimates:

- ✔ **Irregular availability:** Some staff may suddenly be less available than anticipated, so be aware of what their other duties are. If, for example, some of your technical staff are also involved with support, and a major break-down occurs on the production line, they'll suddenly disappear from your project no matter what their per-centage availability is on your plan. If the whole factory has come to a standstill, you can't insist that the staff come back to give their 50 per cent of the week to your project and finish fixing the production line next week.

- ✔ **Multiple staff:** If two or more people are working on a task and must work together on it, then the duration will depend on the one with the least availability. If part of the work can be done without everyone involved, then that impact is reduced.

- ✔ **Project dependencies:** Sometimes, work can't start until staff are released from other work such as work on other projects. And if there's a delay in the other project that will knock on to yours.

- ✔ **Speed of working:** Some staff members perform faster than others, and some organisations perform faster than others.

- ✔ **The team size:** If a task involves a lot of people, they tend to work more slowly than if it just involves two or three people. That's not least because of the communication and organisation needs within the team.

- ✔ **Working environment:** People in some working environ-ments are hassled with noise and interruptions (such as phones ringing). Be realistic in assessing the duration of activities, and don't expect the same productivity from staff in a disruptive environment that you would from the same staff in a peaceful environment where they can focus and work with few distractions or interruptions.

Thinking about productivity

A good estimate is one that's close to how long a task even-tually takes. If the estimates are good, then the project will stick pretty close to the plan and will be a whole lot easier to manage than if it keeps veering wildly off plan.

Defining 'full time'

Being assigned to a project full time doesn't mean a person can perform project work at peak productivity 40 hours per week, 52 weeks per year. During your project, your staff will probably need to read organisational circulars, take holiday, go off sick for a while and, yes, even argue about football occasionally before getting down to the day's work.

So don't ever think of staff as 100 per cent available to the project. The reality is that they won't be, and if you schedule them for five full days a week then your plan won't work. Someone working full time on a project is probably available, on average, four days a week.

 Don't use overtime when planning. Plan using normal working hours only, then if you come under pressure during the project you have overtime working as a fallback. If you've already planned in overtime, you've got nowhere left to run. Also be careful of how you think about overtime. Staff working long hours aren't usually as productive in the overtime hours as they are in the normal ones, because they get tired. But they may not be as productive in the normal hours either. If someone knows he has a really long day ahead, he'll tend to pace himself in the early part of the day.

Making specific adjustments

Where you're basing estimates on how long something took on a previous project in another organisation, or even in another part of your own organisation, you need to factor in productivity. What matters isn't how long it took to do an earlier job *there*, but how long it will take to do the job *here*. So, you may need to make a few adjustments in three areas:

- ✔ Adjusting for the exact nature of the task
- ✔ Adjusting for your people
- ✔ Adjusting for the working environment

The impact of multi-tasking

When someone is working on several tasks at once, the elapsed time of all of them will be increased. The following diagram uses the example of someone switching between three tasks that he's doing at once; you may think, 'Only three things at a time? I wish!'

Each two-week task takes four elapsed weeks

Each two-week task takes two elapsed weeks. A and B are completed earlier and C is no later than before.

If you can organise the work so that people deal with one thing at a time, then the elapsed time of each task will be reduced. If you plan well, you can tell people exactly when you will need them, confirming it as you approach that point so they can clear the decks of other work and so give you faster delivery. As the diagram shows, even just working on one thing at a time gives an improvement, with C being delivered at the same time as before, but A and B both delivered earlier. But even that doesn't account for the extra time needed to pick up the threads if a team member breaks off work on a task and then goes back to it some time later.

For the physical working environment, think about how you might improve it, including ways of working, and so improve productivity. When running projects involving support staff, Nick Graham set up a hot seat system. One person on the team was designated to take all of the support calls for a week. That person would be interrupted frequently, and although he or she did get some project work done, productivity was low. However, the rest of the team were sheltered and could get on without distraction unless a support problem was particularly severe and more help was needed. In the next week, a different team member was in the hot seat, so the hassle was shared out and everyone could work undisturbed most of the time.

Checking historical data

Properly completed time sheets provide the most reliable source of past experience. However, it's with good reason that time sheets are often called 'lie sheets'. Before relying on past metrics, make sure that you fully understand the information, and that includes a careful assessment of the organisational culture, which in turn affects how time is recorded.

Bad time-sheet practices will mean the data is inaccurate:

✔ People aren't allowed to record overtime, so some hours actually spent on an activity may never be known.

✔ People need to send in their time sheets several days before the reporting period is over, so they must guess what their allocations for the next few days will be.

✔ People fill out their time sheets just before they go home at the end of the week. They're in a hurry to get away and can't remember clearly what they did in the early part of the week, so they take a guess and put that down.

✔ People are working on some non-project stuff during the week but are supposed to be allocated full time on the project. So they spread out the hours spent on the other work among your project time codes.

✔ People copy the work-effort estimates from the Project Plan onto their time sheets each period instead of recording the actual number of hours they spend.

If any of these situations exist in your organisation, don't use historical data from time sheets for estimates in your plan.

Smoothing the Resource

The resource conflicts explained in the earlier section 'Dealing with resource conflicts' usually apply to staff. Sometimes, though, you encounter conflicts on things like accommodation or specialised equipment. Physical resource conflicts must dealt with as well as staff resource conflicts.

Checking for resource conflict

To check for resource conflict, you need to look at what each person is scheduled to do in each time period, usually each day. If a person has more to do than there is time available in the day, then there is a resource conflict. That may be because it's a public holiday and there are no working hours that day.

You can create a *Resource Histogram* for each staff member to show any conflicts.Going to back Sue, the overworked team member from earlier in the chapter (see 'Dealing with resource conflicts'), Figure 7-1 shows that Sue is overcommitted and for two days is needed three days per day, which is asking a bit much. To resolve these conflicts, it's necessary to do some *resource smoothing*, sometimes known as resource levelling. The level of required resource needs to be got down below the level of available resource.

Figure 7-1: A Resource Histogram.

Resolving resource conflicts

Here are some straightforward steps for resource smoothing:

1. **Check the activity dependencies and allocations.**

   Continuing the example from the last section, you don't want to solve the problem of Sue being overcommitted if you've put her onto the tasks by mistake and you meant to enter Sam.

2. **Adjust within float.**

   This is where the Activity Network (see Chapter 6) pays dividends. You may see from your network that the latest start date of an activity is considerably further on than the earliest start date, so you can simply slide the activity along within its float to a time when Sue has plenty of availability.

   In Figure 7-1 it looks like the start of Activity A can be delayed as late as Week 9 without causing a problem. However, you'd need to be sure that it doesn't have a knock-on effect. Again, the Activity Network will be really useful, because it shows the dependencies clearly.

3. **Adjust resource.**

   Is there someone else who has the same skill set as Sue? If so and he has more availability at this point, can you assign one or more tasks to him instead? Or alternatively, can you put that person on the task alongside Sue to help; in other words, can you raise the line of available resource?

4. **Move tasks downstream.**

   If you've made changes but still have a resource conflict, you need to move things downstream, and the project end date will go out. In theory, three tasks can be done in parallel, but because of a resource constraint that Sue must do all three, she'll have to do them one after the other, and the impact on the end date is accepted.

Where you have staff who aren't full time on the project, you can sometimes squeeze out a bit more flexibility by talking to them about how they allocate their work. For example, if Sam is available to your project for 50 per cent of his time, that needn't mean he just works mornings. If you have a resource conflict in the early part of a week, you could ask if he could work the first half of the week full time on your project then spend the second half of the week on his other assignments. Involving team members in estimating and resource planning pays off when it comes to asking people to be flexible to meet the needs of both the project and any other assignments.

With all the resourcing issues, the key to success is good plans. If you have clear plans, you not only see the problems but you also have excellent tools to hand to help solve them.

Determining Physical Resource

In addition to staff, your project may require a variety of other important resources. You need to plan for these resources in the same way you plan to meet your staff requirements. As always, when you're planning, you'll often find it helpful to talk to other people, to the point of involving them in a planning workshop.

Identifying resource needs

It's really important to think through *all* the resource requirements for your project and also identify any equipment your organisation already has. Don't forget things such as accommodation and communications equipment for your teams. It's very easy to focus solely on specialised equipment needed to build the project products and so miss important needs in other areas of the project.

Considering availability

It's dangerous to assume that a resource will always be there when you need it, and the more time critical your project is, the more careful you need to be. If you think that sounds a bit like risk management (see Chapter 9), you're right because it overlaps.

Things that can affect physical resource availability include:

- ✔ Bookings from other projects or for operational work
- ✔ Scheduled maintenance

✔ Breakdown and damage

✔ Unforseen needs of a higher priority project

Don't kid yourself that the 'I booked it first' argument will unfailingly hold up in the face of a demand from a top-priority, business-critical project that has the backing of the whole board of directors, the chief constable, the secretary of state or, in the military, someone simply pulling rank.

Making Sense of Budgets

Estimating a project's costs is important for several reasons:

✔ It's a vital element of the Business Case (see Chapter 3) to see whether the project is financially justified.

✔ It allows organisational managers to assess whether the project should be run by comparing the costs against the benefits for this project compared with other 'candidate' projects that could be run instead.

✔ It allows departmental or organisational finance staff to check that the necessary funds are available to support the project, and allocate those funds.

Managing project finance is an essential part of project management and one that's very high profile. If you work in an organisation of any size, you already appreciate just how important finance is. You also know how impressive it is when a Project Manager delivers a project on time, to the required level of quality and also bang on target with the finances.

Looking at different costs

A *project budget* is a time-based estimate of all resource costs for your project. It normally gives a total projected spend for each stage then a total for the whole project. If some of the project's products are to be taken into use during the project, you may also start to see some financial savings during the life of the project. In that case, the budget usually needs to show inbound cash flow as well as outbound.

You typically develop a budget at three points in the project planning. A rough initial estimate when starting up, a full budget when doing the more detailed project planning, then stage budgets in more detail still (if you need them). The project budget is maintained as the project progresses and as better information, including actual costs, becomes available.

Understanding direct and indirect costs

Your project's budget normally includes both direct and indirect costs.

Direct costs are costs for resources solely used for your project. Direct costs include the following:

- Salaries for team members on your project
- Specific materials, supplies and equipment for your project
- Subcontracts that provide support exclusively to your project
- Travel to perform work on your project

Indirect costs are costs for resources that support more than one project but aren't readily identifiable with or chargeable to any of the projects individually. Indirect costs include things such as general services (such as HR) and shared costs that it would be too difficult to allocate to different areas of the business.

It's important to discriminate clearly between the direct and indirect costs – not least because your finance director will! Indirect costs will already be in the organisational budget, but at least some of the direct costs will need to be specially funded.

Understanding capital and revenue

Many organisations refer to costs as capital and revenue. *Revenue* is ongoing year-on-year costs such as building rental, equipment maintenance and staffing. *Capital costs* are one-off purchases such as equipment and contract staff.

Some organisations prefer to use contract staff for at least some of the project work, simply because it can be accounted for as a capital cost whereas recruiting more permanent staff would show up as an ongoing running cost. Higher revenue costs make an organisation appear less efficient because it's spending more on overheads, whereas the staff spend in capital expenditure is hidden. This may seem like political and budgetary manoeuvring, which it is, but be aware of it because it can affect the staffing and funding of your project.

Developing the budget

Organisational decision makers would love to have a detailed and accurate budget on hand whenever someone proposes a project, so they can assess its relative benefits to the organisation and decide whether they have sufficient funds to support it. Unfortunately, you can't prepare such an estimate until you develop a clear understanding of the work and resources the project will require.

Try to resist pressure to state a specific project budget up front before you've done any real thinking about a project. In some organisations, as soon as someone mentions the word *project* ,some finance managers start pushing for a specific project cost. Unfortunately, the finance people then go away and put that figure in the accounts, and just you try changing it now; it's carved in stone. It's for that very reason that the PRIME project management method doesn't use the term 'Business Case' until the more detailed project planning is being done and more reliable costs are to hand.

Developing the rough estimate

In reality, decisions about whether to go forward with the early parts of a project and how to undertake them must be made before people can prepare highly accurate budgets.

The rough, order-of-magnitude estimate is an initial estimate of costs based on a general sense of the project work in the Starting the Project stage. You make this estimate without detailed data. Depending on the nature of the project, the final budget may end up being much more (or less!) than this initial estimate.

You can prepare a rough order-of-magnitude estimate by considering the costs of similar projects (or similar activities that will be part of your project) that have already been done, and applicable cost and productivity information, if you have the luxury of such information being available.

Developing the full budget

In the Organising and Preparing stage you develop the full budget by examining the staff allocations in the plan and checking what you need to buy and use during the project. This budget is approved as part of the full project's approval (it usually forms part of the Project Charter; see Chapter 2) and now provides a baseline against which you can measure project finances. However, even now the budget is not definitive as you still don't know all the fine detail of the project. For example, you don't know at the start of the project exactly what equipment you'll need to buy, because the design hasn't been done yet.

Updating the budget

As you work through the delivery stages, you prepare more-detailed costings as you build successive stage plans and you then update the project-level budget with fresh projections.

Using 'actuals'

Actuals are the information on time actually used on an activity or, in this case, money actually spent. When doing lower, stage level, budgeting and making adjustments you will have the benefit of feedback on the actual time and cost for work done so far. You will also develop formal agreements for the use of equipment, facilities, vendors and other resources so exact costs will be known.

It follows that it's important to keep the budget information up-to-date. You can't use it for checking the current financial position and making projections for the final spend if it is weeks out of date.

Levelling the budget detail

When thinking through the format of your budget, consider who'll be looking at the different parts of it. Typically, the managers who'll approve the project budget won't want to know how many pencil sharpeners you plan to buy in Stage 23 for the user training. An easy approach for budgets is to set them down in three sections, an overview, the full budget and then the detailed item listings.

The item listing can usually be set down in an appendix. It's unlikely that anyone will study this section from end to end, but some people may want to dip in to see how you arrived at a particular figure. In a presentation you'd do well to have the detailed information with you, so if any questions do come up, you can quickly refer to it and be incredibly impressive by coming up with fast, accurate and confident answers.

Monitoring the budget

The point has already been made that the budget must be kept up to date, as must the project plans, in order to be useful as a management tool. With the budget, it's helpful to maintain three figures:

- The planned spend
- The actual spend (on items reached by this point)
- The variance between planned and actual spend

Where the variance is significant, you may need to do some work to investigate why, and even refer it to the steering committee. At worst case, the variance may call the viability of the project into question. However, it is better to identify such a problem and deal with it, to the point of stopping the project, than have the project overspending and out of control.

Chapter 8

Planning at Different Times and Levels

. . . .

In This Chapter

▶ Dividing your project into manageable pieces – the stages

▶ Developing Stage Plans

▶ Deciding on work assignments and making more-detailed plans

. . . .

A great temptation in project planning is to dive into the fine detail and start 'counting rivets' before you're even sure what the project is really about. That's certainly true of planning, and a danger for most people involved in projects is that they go too deep too quickly in planning. The approach in this book, though, is to work at different levels of planning detail at different times.

Here are a few reasons why it makes sense to get the 'helicopter view' before going into detail:

✔ You may be heading in the wrong direction and be doing all sorts of detailed planning on the wrong stuff. It makes sense to check out the high-level before going into detail.

✔ Things change, particularly in business projects. It doesn't make a whole lot of sense to do the detailed planning a long way ahead, because you can be sure that things will have changed by the time you get there and a lot of your work will be wasted.

✔ Until you've seen the bigger picture clearly, you're not going to get the detail right, because you don't properly understand what you're dealing with. For a start, you won't usually be absolutely clear on the scope of the project until the high-level Project Plan is agreed.

The chapters so far in this part cover the sorts of things you do in planning. This chapter brings the earlier chapters together to explain when you plan, at what level, and then how to integrate plans at those different levels of detail.

Putting in the Main Structure

Just about all approaches to project planning and control break the project down into phases or stages. This allows you to concentrate on one part of the project at a time, while still seeing the big picture. Stages also create powerful control points, because between each stage everyone can take stock and check that the project is okay before going on to the next stage. People often refer to these control points as *stage gates*, although if you're working with the PRINCE2 project method you'll see that it still insists on using the unwieldy name of *End Stage Assessment*. You can find more on Stage Gates later in the chapter in 'Holding a Stage Gate'.

Stages are also useful for resource control because they allow managers to drip-feed staff resource and money into the project. Although all the project funds and staff resource are earmarked at the outset, the sponsor or steering committee can specifically authorise the release of that resource one stage at a time, checking on each occasion that the project is still viable and on track.

Deciding on the stages

Two basic sorts of stages exist in projects: management stages and technical stages. *Technical stages* relate to the nature of the project work, so you may have, for example, a design stage and a build stage. In terms of control, though, projects often use management stages. A *management stage* is simply a block of work that the sponsor or steering committee is happy to finance and authorise in one go; a management stage may include several technical stages.

You can think of management stages in exactly the same way as ordinary business management. The sponsor is effectively the boss here, so how much does the boss want to authorise at a time, and how often will she check up on the work being done to make sure everything is okay? Of course, you can't answer the question because it's one that rests on personal judgement. It depends, among other things, on the management style adopted by the boss. A particular boss may exercise quite a lot of control and be happier doing that. However, if another person with a more laid-back management style had been appointed as boss, she might have supervised the same staff much less and checked up less frequently.

The Project Manager may recommend what she thinks is a suitable number of stages for the project and show where they should come, but with management stages it's for the sponsor to decide on the level of control she wants to take.

Here are a few factors to get you thinking:

- **Before a major investment:** If there is a point in the project where a considerable amount of money is to be spent, it makes sense to have a stage gate just before it.

- **Experience of the Project Manager:** Just like in general management, depending on the Project Manager's experience, the boss may want to check up on things more or less often and authorise different amounts at a time.

- **Finance:** Stages are different lengths, but a sponsor may put a cash limit on them. So, the project will cost £12 million, but no stage is ever to be more than £2 million.

- **Risk:** If the project is high risk, a sponsor will tend to want shorter stages so that stage gate checks are more numerous and less is being authorised at a time.

- **Sensible blocks of work:** Sometimes you can almost see the stage boundaries on a plan. The groupings of products and good control points are simply obvious, and it's hard to explain it better than that.

- **Time:** In the same way as for money, the sponsor may put a limit on the maximum length of a stage. In a two-year project, the maximum stage length could be, say, four months. If there is a block of work that will take six months, then it will need to be broken into two stages with a stage gate part-way through that work.

In exactly the same project, a different choice of people on a steering committee or a different choice of sponsor may result in very different decisions on the number of stages in the project.

To get this really clear, have a look at Figure 8-1. For the same project you can see that two different steering committees would choose different patterns of supervision.

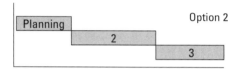

Figure 8-1: Two options for stages of the same project.

Holding a stage gate

The sponsor or steering committee holds the Stage Gate at the end of each stage. The Stage Gate is a look back, a look at where you are now and then a look forward.

- **Looking back:** You look back to check how things went on the stage just finishing. Are there any warning signs that indicate future problems? How much change has there been compared with what was expected? Was the spending on track? What problems came up?

- **Looking at where the project is now:** Is the project still viable and on target to deliver the benefits expected of it? Is the risk is still acceptable?

- **Looking ahead:** You look at the stage ahead and, in particular, the stage level plan. Is that plan workable and achievable? Are the controls adequate? Is the staff resource confirmed to be in place?

If the look back, look at the present position and look ahead are all okay, the Project Manager gets the green light and can go and get on with the next stage.

Working with Planning Levels

You can plan at three different levels:

- ✔ **Project Plan:** Produced by the Project Manager (consulting others) and covering all the delivery stages to give a high level view of the whole project.

- ✔ **Stage Plans:** One for each of the delivery stages. Produced by the Project Manager at the end of the previous stage, just before the new stage commences.

- ✔ **Delivery Plan:** Produced, this time, by a team leader and covering a single work assignment. Sometimes the Stage Plan has sufficient detail to exercise control over the work of a particular assignment and the Team Leader doesn't need a Delivery Plan.

Figure 8-2 shows how the plans fit into the project at the three levels of detail.

Delivery Plans (as and when needed)

Figure 8-2: How plans fit the project.

Drawing up new plans

Stage and Delivery Plans are both drawn up from the level above. Look ahead to Figure 8-3 to see the plans at the three levels. You develop a Stage Plan from the relevant section of the Project Plan, and a team leader develops a Delivery Plan (if needed) for an assignment from the relevant section of the Stage Plan.

Developing a Stage Plan

Developing a Stage Plan from a Project Plan is easy in overall concept, but quite a lot of hard work when it comes to the practicality. The Project Plan shows at a high level what products are being produced in each of the delivery stages – between about 15 and 30 products.

When you're approaching a Stage Gate, it's time to start thinking about the Stage Plan for the following stage and identify the high-level, project-level, products for that stage. There may be two or three of them; it rather depends on the size of your project.

You then break these two or three products down in detail, normally using a Work Breakdown Structure, until you again have 15–30. For these you draw a Work Flow Diagram and then go on to show the greater detail of activities in your activity network and Gantt Chart. You can find full detail of all these techniques in Chapters 5 to 7.

Developing a Delivery Plan

Of the 15–30 stage-level products, a work assignment or *Work Package* to be given to a team leader may comprise two or three of them or just a single product. Then exactly the same planning sequence is used all over again, but this time at an even lower level of detail.

Planning for resource and budget

In exactly the same way as the product and activity plans show more detail at stage and then Work Package levels, you now go into more detail in your resource planning, including for financial resource. Figure 8-3 shows this graphically.

Figure 8-3: Plan types and levels.

Figure 8-4 summarises what plans you'll be producing during the life of your project and when.

Figure 8-4: Planning points in a project.

Keeping higher level plans up to date

When lower-level plans are produced, it is common to find some things that weren't seen on the higher-level ones and to come up with better information such as on activity durations. Each higher-level plan should be updated as necessary from what is discovered when doing the lower-level planning.

Planning at more than one level at once

Just occasionally, you may want go against the 'just in time' approach to planning in which you plan just before that plan is required; you draw up a Stage Plan towards the end of the previous stage. For example, in larger projects, you may ask suppliers to draw up Delivery Plans for their parts of the work in a forthcoming stage, and then build the Stage Plan from the Delivery Plans.

As in all areas of project planning, be flexible and do what's best for the project. The important thing is always doing what's best to get the job done.

Wellington attributed his success against Napoleon to flexibility. He said that Napoleon's battle plans were made of gold and fine jewels. Napoleon thought through and planned battles very carefully in advance. If the battle went the way he had envisaged, things generally went well for him, but if not he was in trouble. Wellington described his battle plans as being made of rope. If something snapped, he just tied a knot and carried on.

Chapter 9

Managing the Risk

*I*t's sad to hear about good projects that have failed – but it happens. It's even sadder when you find out a bit more and see that a project was killed off by a problem that the Project Manager could easily have foreseen, controlled or even prevented. Don't let your project be unnecessarily damaged or even destroyed by something that with a bit of effort – and sometimes not that much effort – you can get a handle on. This is the realm of risk management. The good news is that the basics aren't that difficult; in fact, you do risk management nearly all the time just to get through the day.

All projects need risk management, even the very small ones. However, some projects are clearly higher risk than others and justify more effort. Often the larger, more complex and longer your project is, the more risk management you need, but that doesn't let small projects off the hook. The highest-commercial-risk project Nick Graham has ever encountered was also one of the smallest: a six-week project with just two staff in a finance company in the City of London. If that project had failed, it would have seriously damaged the company's reputation in the City and threatened its whole business.

This chapter discusses risk, how to identify risks, assess the impacts, and then plan and take action to control risks.

Understanding Risk

Risk is the possibility that you may not achieve some or all of your objectives because something unexpected occurs or something planned doesn't occur. All projects have some degree of risk but the risk is generally greater:

- ✔ The longer your project lasts

- ✔ The more unusual and groundbreaking the project is

- ✔ The less experience you, your organisation or your team members have with the type of project

- ✔ The more vulnerable the project is to things happening outside (such as in the wider business or due to change of government policy, change in the marketplace, activity of competitors or dependency on other projects)

- ✔ The newer your project's technology is

The current professional view of risk in projects is that it's about uncertainty, and that individual risks can be either positive or negative:

- ✔ *Negative risks*, also referred to as *downside risks* or *threats*, potentially have a detrimental effect on one or more of the project objectives, such as causing you to miss a deadline.

- ✔ *Positive risks*, also referred to as *upside risk* or *opportunities*, potentially have a beneficial effect on project objectives, such as allowing you to complete a task with fewer staff than you originally planned.

Seeing why you need risk management

Risk in projects is mostly negative – things that can go wrong – so this chapter focuses mostly on that. The negative view is in line with dictionary definitions of risk, of which one is: 'The adverse consequences of future events.'

Obviously, wherever you can, you want to try to stop things going wrong, and so increase the chances of success. Risk management can get complicated in high-risk projects, but for most it isn't going to be difficult, and for many it's straight-forward. The important thing is that you must manage risks unless you want to open the project to the possibility of costly damage and even failure, when you might have been able to take a simple action to control it. It's been said that the right question isn't 'Should we do risk management?' but rather 'How much risk management should we do?'

On low risk projects you may not do much risk management, but you should always do some. For some projects, that may just mean gathering one or two people together for 20 min-utes around a flip chart to look at what could go wrong with the project and how that might be controlled.

Don't think that small projects don't need risk management. In some respects, small projects are inherently high risk. Take staffing, for example. If someone leaves your project and you have 200 people, the impact is about 0.5 per cent (it may be more or less depending on how important that person's job is). If there's just you and one other person and the other person leaves, the impact is magnified: it's 50 per cent.

Managing risk

It's important to take on board the exact wording of the sub-ject area of this chapter, which is risk *management.* Managing risk doesn't necessarily mean avoiding it. Clearly, a positive risk (an upside risk) is something that you want to happen, and your management action includes making it more likely. However, even negative risk may be a good option in the proj-ect if the gain, such as time saving, is worthwhile.

You should manage and communicate project risks from the beginning and regularly. In particular, share information at the following points in your project (see Chapter 2 for more about these project stages):

- ✔ **Starting the Project:** To support the process of deciding whether to undertake the project

- ✔ **Organising and Preparing:** To guide the development of all aspects of your Project Plan

- ✔ **Carrying Out the Work:** To regularly review risks and deal with any new ones found.

Within the project you can discuss this information at regularly scheduled meetings such as with the steering committee or project board.

Working Through the Risk Cycle

A cycle gives a framework to show how you analyse, decide actions and then manage the risks that may affect a project.

Different approaches to risk management offer different cycles. The example in Figure 9-1 is from Inspirandum's publication *The Project Techniques Toolbox*.

As shown in Figure 9-1, the steps after the initial identification of a risk go on continually, with regular review, right through the project. Clearly, if something about the risk has changed, such as it has become more severe, you may need to make changes in the way that you're handling that risk. It could be that a course of action that wasn't justified when the risk was low severity is now fully justified because the risk has become high severity.

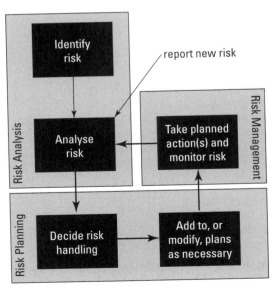

Figure 9-1: A risk cycle example.

Here's an outline of the steps in the cycle:

1. **Identify risks.**

   Determine what the risks are that may affect your project. You want to look at things within the project but also things that can come in from outside. During the project, in particular, some new risks may also be reported to you by people involved in the project.

2. **Analyse risks.**

   This is where you get to grips with each risk to make sure you really understand it. You normally put some measures on each risk such as the probability of the risk happening and the impact if it does.

3. **Decide risk handling.**

   Here you think how you can protect your project from negative risk while trying to take advantage of positive risks. For some risks you may decide not to take any action, but that's still a decision.

4. **Add to or modify plans as necessary.**

   Having decided what to do, if action is needed you're going to have to build that into the plan. For example, there may be risk actions that you'll need to include in the activity plans (see Chapter 6 for more on activity planning). Because this step is part of the cycle, you may already have some management actions planned for a particular risk, so in this step you adjust the action to reflect any changes you've decided on.

5. **Take planned action(s) and monitor risk.**

   There's no point in planning actions if you don't take them, so this step is to take action, either as an ongoing action or as a response if the risk happens. You also monitor each risk to see whether it's changing and to check that any action is effective. If the action is proving insufficient or the risk has changed, the cycle goes back to step 2 to re-analyse the risk, and then on around the cycle again to decide how the risk handling should be changed.

The following sections look at each step in more detail.

Identifying risk

The first step is to identify the risks. You should record these in a *Risk Register*, which is simply a set of forms, each one describing a risk. Don't think of the Risk Register as bureaucratic, because you've got to be able to refer back to the information, and you can't do that if you don't record it.

Identification isn't a repeatable part of the cycle, but remember that you will need check for new risks periodically. This may be at the end of each stage or at regular intervals.

The good thing about risk management is that there are lots of techniques out there to help (including Inspirandum's *The Project Techniques Toolbox*). You can also find details of four techniques in the 'Getting Some Help from Techniques' section at the end of this chapter..

Introducing a structure

You can just think of risks at random, but you may find it helpful to bring in some structure. For example, you may think about risks in terms of the type of impact or in categories. Categories can also be helpful to help decide how the risk should be handled and by whom.

Different organisations and project and risk approaches use different sets of risk categories, and you can look on the Internet to find a few. You'll find two simple examples, PESTLE and BPEST, in the nearby sidebar 'Risk categories'.

Risk categories

Some sets of risk category are quite long and complicated, and others relate to specific business areas such as insurance or construction. Here are a couple of simple category sets that are widely used in organisational risk management but that you can also use in projects.

PESTLE	**BPEST**
Political	Business
Economic	Political
Social	Economic
Technological	Social
Legal	Technological
Environmental	

Looking around for help

Don't think you always have to do everything yourself. With risk in particular, it really helps to get different viewpoints, because different people will spot risks that you don't.

Here are a few ideas on finding help to get you started:

- ✔ **Review past records of problems encountered in similar situations.** If a risk materialised on a similar project in the past, you want to be prepared for it.

- ✔ **Brainstorm with experts and other people who have related experiences.** The more sources of expert opinion you consult, the less chance you have of overlooking something. Here a risk workshop can be very effective.

- ✔ **Use a Risk Checklist.** You'll find more on this technique in the later section 'Risk Checklist', but basically it's a standard list of risks that you can look through. See whether any risks on the list could affect your project.

- ✔ **Look on the Internet.** It's surprising what a quick surf can turn up.

Analysing risk

The second step in the risk cycle is analysis, when you get to really understand a risk. You need to know what can cause the risk, how it is likely to behave, what its impact will be and if it is related to any other risks. In projects people often think about individual risks but fail to consider the possibility of relationships between them. A single event may fire off several risks at once, or cause a chain reaction when one risk happening fires off another risk, and so on.

As part of your analysis, it's really helpful to assess the scale of the risk and when it can happen. In turn, that helps you think how much management of the risk you need to do, which is important because risk management will itself take time in the project and possibly cost money. The scales are normally in two dimensions – probability and impact – and you can use a Probability–Impact (P-I) Grid diagram to help (see Figure 9-2 for an example).

Differentiating between risks and impacts

When looking for risks, it's really easy to confuse risks and impacts. For example, a common entry in Risk Registers is: 'RISK 99 – Project will be delayed'. However, delay isn't a risk, it's an impact. What you need to ask is what could go wrong in the project that would result in the project being delayed. So, a major machinery breakdown in the factory during your project could lead to the impact of project delay, because the engineers on your team will be taken off their project work to deal with the breakdown, and will only come back when it's sorted out. Equally, overspending is an impact not a risk. You need to identify any risks that would cause overspending.

Risk experts recommend that you use a scale of at least five, even if you don't use numbers (you can use very high, high, medium, low and very low). On the other hand, don't go for a scale of more than ten, or you start to get into difficulties about whether the risk is a 678 or if it tips the balance and really justifies a 679 on your 1,000-point scale.

VH, H, M, L, VL
or numbers 1-5 or 1-10

Risk 1: 1 x 1 = 1
Risk 2: 2 x 2 = 4
Risk 3: 1 x 5 = 5
Risk 4: 5 x 1 = 5
Risk 5: 5 x 5 = not good at all!

Figure 9-2: The Probability–Impact Grid.

The P-I Grid is valuable to see where individual risks are, but also to spot patterns. You might see, for example, that although you have a lot of risks, they are mostly low probability but high impact, or that the risks are evenly scattered across the grid.

When you have the position of each risk worked out, you can use this to help determine what action you need to take. Generally, the more you go towards the top right of the grid, the more action you need to consider. However, this isn't a numbers game, so be careful – particularly in the top left and bottom right of the grid. In Figure 9-2, Risk 3 is very low impact but very high probability. You need to take action, even though its overall score, multiplying the impact scale by the probability scale, is only 5 (1×5). Equally, Risk 4 probably justifies action. It's only got a severity rating of 5 (5×1) but while it's very low probability, its impact would be devastating.

The grid is also useful for regular risk reporting, and you can show any movement of a risk since the last reporting point with dotted lines. In Figure 9-2, you can see that Risks 1 and 5 have changed since the last reporting point, but the others still have the same evaluation of impact and probability.

Gauging probability

Probability can be expressed as a number between 0 and 1, with 0.0 signifying that a situation will never happen, and 1.0 signifying that it will always occur. You may also express probability as a percentage, with 100 per cent meaning the situation will always occur.

You don't have to use the P-I Grid for recording probability and impact though and you can simply list the risks

If you have objective data on the number of times a risk has occurred in similar situations in the past, you can use it to help determine the likelihood that the risk will occur again in the future. However, don't be surprised if you don't have such information, because most risk probability estimates just aren't like that. The lack of data makes the probability estimating difficult; it's been described as the Achilles Heel of risk management.

Where you don't have objective data available, you can use personal judgements to estimate the likelihood that a risk will occur. One technique that can help is the Delphi technique, described at the end of Chapter 6 in the context of estimating activity durations. Try to get the opinions of experts and people who've worked on similar projects in the past.

Areas of impact

When thinking about impact, you need to think widely and include:

✔ Business Case and the level of business benefits

✔ Cost

✔ Corporate targets

✔ Other projects (inter-project dependencies)

✔ Reputation damage (often under-estimated)

✔ Resource scheduling

✔ Time

Estimating the impact

After you identify the likelihood that a particular risk will affect your project, be sure to determine the impact if the risk does occur. That magnitude directly influences how you will decide to deal with the risk. Determine the specific effect that each risk may have on your project's product, schedule and resource performance. When evaluating these effects:

✔ **Consider the effect of a risk on the total project.** Taking one week longer than you planned to complete an activity may cause you to miss intermediate milestones. However, the effect on the project is even greater if the delayed activity is on your project's critical path (see Chapter 6), which means the delay on that one activity also causes a week-long delay for your entire project.

✔ **Consider the combined effect of related risks.** The likelihood that your schedule will slip is greater if three activities on the critical path each has a risk with a significant impact of delay, rather than just one.

Being specific

Be sure to describe risks and their associated consequences as specifically as possible. It the impact is delay, are you talking about one day? One month?

Deciding on an impact scale

The scale for impact in particular is one that you or your organisation as a whole must decide, because it's relative to the organisation. For example, take an impact of a loss of £1 million. Is that a problem? Well, to a small business with just three employees, that isn't just 'very high' – it's a company killer and off the scale completely. However for a multinational company with a multi billion pound turnover it may be little more than an embarrassment and an irritation.

Considering proximity

A third useful measure for each risk, after probability and impact, is the *proximity*: how soon it can happen. Proximity information is, obviously enough, very useful in planning. Three types of proximity exist:

- **Immediate:** Some risks always have a proximity of *now*, because they can happen at any time during the project with no notice at all. An easy example is with a key team member going sick. He may walk up to you in five minutes' time and say that he's feeling dreadful and needs to go home, or that could happen in five weeks' time or in five months' time.

- **Fixed date:** Some risks are pegged to a point in time. The new rocket can't fail to launch until it's time to launch it. The team can't find that a product is more complicated to build than they thought, and so will take longer, until they get to grips with the product as they start to build it.

- **Fixed period:** Some risks will always happen a certain time ahead. Today the proximity of a particular risk is four weeks, but in five months' time the proximity of the risk will still be four weeks. That sounds weird until you consider the simple example of someone resigning from your organisation and so leaving your project. If that person resigns today, he'll leave in four weeks' time, after he's worked his four-week notice period. If he resigns in five months' time, he'll leave four weeks after that. You just hope that he doesn't have four weeks' holiday owing and a fixed period turns into now! You might even decide to check that out.

Deciding risk handling

Recognising and evaluating risks that pose a threat to your project are the first steps towards control. But you can't stop there. You also have to develop specific plans for reducing their potential negative effects on your project. You start by deciding the options available for dealing with each one, and then select the option or options that are most suitable.

Handling all risks

As you look at the risks, be clear on the point that you're going to manage all of them, even if your choice of action for some may be to do nothing. That may sound more than a little strange until you think back to the risk cycle. As the risk goes into the management part of the cycle, you monitor it to check for changes. It may be that a risk where you decided to take no action has now changed and now does justify action. So you're still managing a 'do nothing' risk because you will continue to monitor it.

For example, in London you identify a risk to your project: you won't be able to recruit enough bricklayers when you get to the construction phase of your large new headquarters building on the banks of the River Thames. However, you decide that you don't need to take action, because there's no reported shortage of bricklayers in London and you've budgeted for the going rate of pay. Then, after the project starts and the initial design work is going on, you hear that London has won the bid for the 2012 Olympics and a huge amount of early construction work will be kicking off on the Olympic sites just as you'll be approaching the brickwork part of your project. The circumstances surrounding that risk have changed, and doing nothing is no longer a sensible way of dealing with the risk.

Thinking wide

When considering what to do about each risk, it's very easy to bounce off at a superficial level, and Project Managers often come up with a single option: throw money at the risk. But often you can do a number of things to manage a risk, and some may not involve money at all, just some ingenuity. Allowing sufficient time for risk analysis and management is important, then, so that you don't just rush into the obvious management actions that may not be the cheapest or even the most effective.

Record all the risk management options for each risk, albeit as concisely as possible, and include the reasons for choosing the actions that are being taken and the reasons for not selecting the others. That way, if circumstances change later on and it's necessary to review the decision, the original information is still to hand. That information saves you repeating work that you've already done.

Deciding on actions

When making a decision on what action(s) to take, first consider the likelihood of a risk *and* its potential effect on your project. If the potential effect of a risk is great, and if the chances it will occur are high, you probably want to develop plans to manage that risk. If both the impact and the probability are low (bottom left of the P-I Grid; see the section 'Analysing risk'), you may decide not to take action.

Understanding action types

You can categorise options for handling risks in different ways, but here are five main alternatives:

- ✔ **Avoidance:** Act to stop the risk happening. An example is deciding not to use a new, untested procedure that you're concerned may not produce the desired project results.

- ✔ **Contingency:** This is allowing for the risk to happen, so that you can absorb the impact. Three sub-types of contingency exist:

  - • **Action contingency:** Have a plan B. If the risk is realised, take the pre-planned alternative action. If the flight to Edinburgh is cancelled because of volcanic dust from Iceland, I'll go by train.

  - • **Cost contingency:** Have some extra money in a risk budget. If the supply from the cheaper source fails, the relevant part of the risk budget is released and the item can be purchased from a better stocked but more expensive supplier.

  - • **Time contingency:** Allow some contingency time in your plan to allow for a few deliveries to be late.

- ✔ **Mitigation:** To reduce the probability that a risk will occur or to minimise the impact if it does occur. Two examples of risk mitigation are:

  - • **Minimise the probability.** Use only experienced staff on the project and so reduce the chance of serious mistakes being made.

- Minimise the impact. Have a spare engineer identified who, alongside her normal work, will attend all the project briefings and be copied in on project engineering documents. That way, if someone leaves the engineering team suddenly, this spare person can step in and join the project as a replacement. He'll still have a learning curve, but it's less steep than if he knew nothing about the project at all. He'll get up to speed faster, and the impact of the staff change will be reduced.

✔ **Taking no action:** This is a conscious, and recorded, decision not to take action on the risk; it isn't neglect. If the risk does occur, everyone knew what the impact would be. You might use this option if taking action is very expensive or time consuming, and the low impact and very low probability of the risk occurring doesn't justify such cost or work effort.

✔ **Transfer:** Get someone else to take as much of the risk as possible. For example, take out insurance to cover the financial impact.

You can use the action types in combination. For example, you might choose to have some contingency in the plan to deal with a time delay, but also take out insurance (transfer) to cover the financial impact.

We don't recommend the following risk approaches, even though they are in widespread use – particularly by senior managers:

✔ **The denial approach:** Refusing to accept that any 'real' risks are associated with the project work

✔ **The ostrich approach:** Ignoring all risks, pretending they don't exist

✔ **The prayer approach:** Looking to a higher being to solve the problems and make the risks disappear

Positive risks generally need the opposite action from negative risks. Instead of trying to reduce a risk, you need to take measures to increase the chances of the risk happening and improve the effects if it does. An exception is with taking no action. Even though a risk has a beneficial outcome, it may not be worth the extra effort trying to bring it about.

Modifying plans as necessary

Having decided risk management actions you need to build those actions into the plans and treat them like any other project management work. Where something has changed on a risk that is already known about and for which actions are planned or are already being taken, you need to modify those actions, depending on the review of what's now needed.

Conceptually, this step is simple enough. But do be aware that putting in the risk actions may then affect the overall plan. You'll need to make allowances for risk activity when first drafting the plan out, but later in the project risk activity could even lead to a significant update of the plan. In particular the risk management actions may change costs and timings. They may also have knock on effects, such as affecting the schedule for delivery of products during the project. In turn that may affect other projects if they need those deliverables too because of an inter-project dependency

In addition to the work on individual risk actions, there is also work to be put on the plan for the Project Manager (and perhaps others too) in order to regularly review risks and keep the risk documentation up to date. How much work is involved and how often depends partly on the criticality of the project and partly on the number of risks involved. In a very high-risk project, review will be more frequent than in a low risk project.

Taking planned actions and monitoring risk

At the start of this chapter the point was made that it's sad when a project fails because something nasty happens that could easily have been identified up front and which could have been controlled or even prevented. It's even sadder when risks were identified, actions planned, but then the project dies because those actions were never taken. Risks happened with nothing to control them and killed the project.

This final step of the risk cycle is essential, obviously, and to be sure that it is done, it can be included in regular health checks. You normally do this checking in a project audit function (see Chapter 10). That check isn't merely on the Project Manager, though. If team members, or even the sponsor, are supposed to be taking risk-related action, project audit will check that they are and sound the alarm bells if it's being overlooked.

Taking action on risk

Risk action may be continuous or it may be responsive if the risk actually happens. If the building catches fire, then someone is designated to call the fire brigade; that's a responsive action if the risk occurs. Other risks may need ongoing action, particularly but not solely actions to avoid or reduce risk. So every Friday you jump out of your seat in shock at midday, despite the reminder notice in the lift, because the fire alarm system is being tested to reduce the risk of it not functioning in an emergency.

Monitoring risks

Risks should be monitored regularly and in two dimensions:

- **For change:** Has the risk increased in probability? Is the impact less than expected? Has the timing changed? Any change means that the risk needs to be re-assessed and, if necessary, the control actions changed. That's where this step cycles around to the analysing risk step.

- **For adequacy of the action(s):** Where actions are being taken, are they working? If not, they need to be re-considered, which in turn means that some re-analysis may be helpful: something may have been missed which led to the wrong actions being selected in the first place. The cycle continues with a link back to analysing risk.

Documenting Risk

Two key documents are involved with risk management, and in all but very small projects these are both necessary and important. Even a small project should have some means of risk recording, though. The two documents are a *risk management plan* and a *Risk Register*.

Risk Management Plan

A *risk management plan* lays out the strategy for how risk will be managed in your project. Develop your risk management plan in the Organising and Preparing stage of your project, refine it as necessary at the end of each stage when planning the next stage, and continually update it where needed during stages (see Chapter 2 for more on these stages). Include the following in your risk-management plan:

- Communications and interfaces, such as with programme management or other projects that may be affected

- How risk actions will be monitored and audited

- Reporting mechanisms, such as how team members should report newly discovered risks and how they should say if they believe a risk is starting to happen

- Review points where risk will be re-assessed, such as at the end of each stage and at regular monthly intervals during each stage, unless it's getting near an end stage

- Scales to be used, such as the impact scale

- Your plan for keeping people informed about risks throughout the project

Risk Register

You need a *Risk Register* or *Risk Log* in which to record risks, the action being taken on them and the responsibilities for managing each one.

The Risk Register holds the day-to-day control information for each risk that's been identified. You can adjust the contents to meet the exact needs of your project but, as always, try to keep things simple. At a minimum, you're likely to need the following information:

- **ID:** Usually a number

- **Risk title:** A short name to identify the risk quickly

- **Status:** Whether the risk is increasing, decreasing, stable, under review or dead

✔ **Description:** A full description covering the characteristics of the risk and how it is likely to behave, such as whether it may happen gradually or instantly

✔ **Metrics:** Impact, probability and proximity information

✔ **Responsibilities:** Who's responsible for the risk, including taking any action on it

✔ **Notifier:** Who spotted the risk in the first place (that might be a good person consult if there are changes)

✔ **Planned actions:** What actions will be taken to control the risk, or that it has been decided not to take action

Make the Risk Register available so people can see it and try. not to hide risk. With supplier staff it's better to get non-disclosure agreements than to hide risk. Some confidential information can't be made available, but hiding things unnecessarily is itself a risk.

Using Risk Techniques

The good thing about risk management is that there are lots of techniques to help. In this last section you'll find four basic ones to get you started.

Ishikawa (fishbone) diagram

The fishbone diagram is useful when you want to work through risk identification in a structured way. You can do this using one impact at a time, such as 'delay' or 'overspending'. Figure 9-3 gives an example with a partially completed diagram.

Work Flow Diagram

The Work Flow Diagram, explained in Chapter 5, shows all the project's products in sequence, including those coming into the project from outside. This gives a natural structure for part of the risk analysis. Simply go through the project products one at a time asking 'What could go wrong with producing this product or with this external supply?'

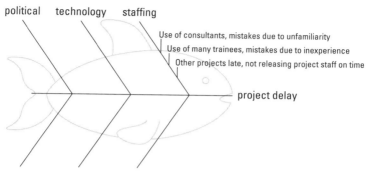

political   technology   staffing

Use of consultants, mistakes due to unfamiliarity

Use of many trainees, mistakes due to inexperience

Other projects late, not releasing project staff on time

project delay

Figure 9-3: The Ishikawa (fishbone) diagram.

Risk Checklist

The risk checklist is simply a standard list of known risks grouped by category. You can buy commercial ones, but making your own is even better. You identify all the risks you can by using other techniques, and then use the checklist to see if you've missed anything. Don't use the checklist first, or you're likely to get focused on it and so miss a new risk that's staring you in the face but isn't on the list.

Decision Tree

A decision tree allows you to map options and cost them against the probability of them occurring. The result helps indicate the best action. Figure 9-4 gives an example with two main choices of supplier. The actual cost for each then depends on whether that supplier delivers on time, early (in which case they get a bonus payment) or late (in which case there is a deduction from the cost for the inconvenience). The known history of the two suppliers allows estimation of the probability of each being early, on time or late.

This analysis suggests that you can expect to pay supplier A £45,000 and have a 70 per cent chance of delivery on time or early. You can expect to pay vendor B £56,000 and have a 70 per cent chance of delivery on time or early. So you can see that vendor A is the better choice.

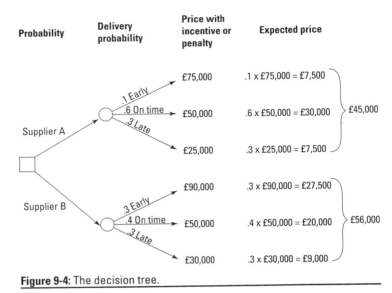

Figure 9-4: The decision tree.

Part III
Putting Your Management Team Together

'I-NEED-A-BIGGER-BUDGET-FOR-MY-PROJECT!!'

In this part . . .

The key to successful projects is people – using their capabilities to the fullest, encouraging their mutually supportive work efforts and sustaining their ongoing commitment to your project's success.

This part looks at the organisational structure of a project, sets down clear roles and responsibilities, examines the impact of good and bad leadership and discusses how to get the best out of teams.

Chapter 10

Organising the Project

*I*n a project, clear organisation is vital. A commonly reported cause of project problems and project failure is unclear roles and responsibilities. This chapter helps you pin down very clear roles and responsibilities. To get any job done involving more people than just you, some organisation is needed. You need to know who's doing what, who's in charge and who's responsible for different aspects of the work.

This chapter explores project organisation, shows some different options for it and give some hints and tips for getting it right. Getting the right organisation is important for your project for two reasons. First, if you have unclear roles and responsibilities, you're going to get communications breakdowns and misunderstandings. Second, if the structure doesn't fit the project properly – for example, if you have a big structure that requires an expensive meeting and lots of people to make a minor decision – you're likely to get delays and excessive overheads.

Some organisations are becoming 'projectised', that is the structure of the organisation is being changed to fit around a project way of working. Some companies now have a dedicated projects department, while others have adopted something known as *Matrix Management*. The chapter will help you understand the organisational context of your project and will explain variants you may come across in the future, if you haven't already.

Designing the Project Structure

In a small project, the organisation may be very simple with just a sponsor who's the manager who wants the project and is paying for it, a Project Manager who often does some of the project work alongside managing it, and then perhaps one or two more people who help with the work as team members. Figure 10-1 illustrates a simple organisation structure.

Figure 10-1: A simple organisation structure for a small project.

In Figure 10-1 only three people are involved in the project. Cheng is the manager in overall charge of the project and takes the role of sponsor. Sep is the Project Manager running the project day to day, but is also doing some of the project work himself so is also taking the role of a team member alongside his project management work. Anne is a technical specialist who's in the project as a team member, and she's working with Sep on the technical work.

In a bigger project, you may well have a project board or steering committee in overall charge, a Project Manager who is full time in that role, and then a number of teams from inside the organisation and some teams from outside suppliers, each with a team leader.

You may need to fight a bit – politely of course – to get an appropriate structure for your project. If your organisation has a standard organisation structure for its projects, geared to satisfy the needs of large projects, it's almost certainly going to be excessive if your project is small. It may take some effort to convince organisational managers that your project should have a simpler, smaller structure, but that effort will be repaid when you don't have to deal with an unwieldy structure right through the project. One way to help sell your argument is by showing that the project will have lower overheads.

Understanding roles

People often talk about 'roles and responsibilities' without thinking too much about the phrase. In projects, though, the word *role* is very significant and also very helpful when you're designing the organisation of a particular project. The word is significant for three reasons:

- ✔ **One person (job) can have more than one role.** In smaller projects especially, one person's 'job' on the project could be made up of a couple of roles. An example is given in Figure 10-1 where Sep is the Project Manager but is also doing some of the work of the project. When he's doing technical project work, Sep is a team member. But when he's managing the project, he's a Project Manager. So Sep wears two hats: he's got two roles; for some of his time he's a Project Manager and for the rest of his time he's a team member.

- ✔ **Some roles can be shared by more than one person.** If there's a role on your steering committee for a user manager representative to make sure the project is delivering things that the user staff can operate, then that role can be split between two people. For example, if the project is delivering things that will affect staff in two operational departments, you may want a manager from each department to sit on the committee to make sure the deliverables are okay for each department's people. So two managers fill the one role of user representative.

✔ **Roles emphasise function and not status.** Project work isn't about status – how important someone is in the organisation – but function. Project organisation can turn normal reporting lines completely upside down. The Project Manager may be a relatively junior manager in the organisation, and one of the teams may have a very senior legal adviser on it. So in the project, a very senior manager may be accountable to someone who's much more junior in terms of grade.

Nick Graham has provided project training and consultancy advice to a number of UK police forces. UK police forces are very 'command and control' orientated, and in many cases more so than the military, so someone's rank is extremely important. One project involved significant change in force policy and, because of this, two of the team members were the deputy chief constable and the director of human resources (the most senior civilian grade in the force). The Project Manager was a police inspector (two hops up from the bottom grade: constable to sergeant to inspector). The normal reporting lines were turned completely upside down in the project, and a team member who was the deputy chief constable was accountable to the Project Manager who was an inspector. That's okay, though. Project roles are about function not status, and the police officers involved fully understood that.

Getting to grips with roles

Where your project is more than a very small one, you're going to need a more sophisticated organisation structure. Do be careful in your thinking when you do the work to set this up, though. Always keep the structure as simple as possible.

Figure 10-2 outlines the roles. You can have all of the roles filled with relatively few people if you need to. You can get models for project structure from many places, but this example comes from the PRIME project methodology (more on this in Chapter 2). Although you can see that this is more detailed than the simple example in Figure 10-1, it's also very flexible.

From the PRIME method; used with permission.

Figure 10-2: An example of project organisation.

The PRIME approach is very flexible partly because it uses roles but also because it allows extra roles to be added to the organisation structure where you need them. In many methods, such as PRINCE2 (also see Chapter 2), the approach is presented in its full complexity in the manual, and you have to simplify it where you can. PRIME starts at the other end and sets out to keep things simple, which is fine for most projects, but where you need extra power for something more substantial, you can add in one or more PowerPacks. The PRIME PowerPacks provide more sophisticated content, such as for high-risk projects, and are relevant here because they can affect the roles. The High Risk PowerPack, for example, gives the option of adding a dedicated project risk manager into the top management of the project, and you see that in the 'optional power roles' box in Figure 10-2.

Looking at the roles

This section explains the roles as set down in the example in Figure 10-1, but don't worry if you use a different method or none at all. The principles hold good whatever environment you're working in.

Project management team

This is the top management team of the project. In a smaller project, you may have a single sponsor taking all the roles except Project Manager (see the later section about sponsors). You may know the top management group as a *project steering committee* or *project board*.

Project director

If the project was a temporary department in the organisation, then this role would be the head of department. The *project director* is supported by other senior managers in the project management team, but is the manager ultimately responsible for the project. This position makes sense. Taking the analogy of a project as being like a temporary department, you have one person in overall charge of it.

This role can't be shared. Don't ever have a committee, for example, as project director. All members of the project management team are responsible for making sure that the project is viable, but the project director has specific, final and personal responsibility for it.

The project director needs to understand both projects and business, of course, but must also have sufficient authority to take decisions, and preferably some enthusiasm, charisma and leadership qualities to provide drive within the project. A bored and uninterested project director isn't going to inspire enthusiasm and hard work within the teams.

Sponsor

The *sponsor* is the person who wants the project and whose staff will be using whatever the project is delivering. The sponsor is there to provide a strong link between the project and the staff in the operational area. The sponsor also provides any business staff who are needed on project teams to help specify what is needed, and perhaps to help test final products to make sure that they're okay for operational use.

PRIME uses the term *sponsor* to describe the person representing the business area that will use what the project is delivering. The person in overall charge is the project director. However, and confusingly when reading a book about project management, terms are not used consistently across organisations or even across project approaches. You may not have project directors in your organisation but have a single person who's both representing the user area and in overall charge of the project, who you refer to as the sponsor. That's very common and the usage through most of this book. PRIME is a bit more specific and so discriminates clearly between the two functions with two separate roles.

Provider

The *provider* provides the technical staff resource for the project – the teams. The provider must have the authority to commit that resource, or get that authority from others. You don't want the Project Manager running around trying to persuade people to take part – especially if that Project Manager is you. Rather, you have a provider who has the organisational authority to commit resource. If the project involves a major outside supplier company working on the project alongside organisational staff, you'll probably want to have two people in the role. The provider from your own organisation will authorise internal staff resource, and the provider from the supplier company will authorise staff resource from that company.

Project Manager

The *Project Manager* takes day-to-day responsibility for managing the project on behalf of the full project management team. The Project Manager has specific responsibilities to plan the project, control it and manage the staff resource. Normally a project has a number of teams, so the direct team management will be done by team leaders, but the Project Manager still has an important function to motivate and direct the project staff.

In addition to the main elements of planning and control, the Project Manager must also deal with problems and changes, referring to the full project management team anything that is beyond his delegated authority.

Only have one Project Manager – just one person in the role. Some organisations break that rule and have a 'Business Project Manager' and a 'Technical Project Manager', for example. Splitting the role in two (or more) isn't a good idea though, because neither person is a 'project' manager by definition, because she doesn't have a view of the whole project, only a part of it. There's a danger of things dropping down the gap if neither person saw it or one person saw it but assumed that the other person was dealing with it. In really bad cases, the two Project Managers can come to loggerheads – and yes, it's been known! If you want a powerful analogy of this idea in another area of management, try a ship. Even huge passenger liners and oil tankers have only one captain when they're on a voyage, and for the same management reason as in a project: one person knows what's going on.

Keep your project management team, steering committee or project board small; preferably with a maximum of six people. Big management groups don't ever meet – there's always someone unable to make the meeting and usually several. Big management groups tend to be a big problem in organisations using PRINCE2, and if you'd like advice on how to keep a PRINCE2 project board scaled down and working properly, it's worth investing in a copy of *PRINCE2 For Dummies* by Nick Graham (Wiley), in which you'll find a whole chapter on running project boards successfully.

Project audit

It makes sense to have the project checked now and then to be sure that everything's okay. *Project audit* does that checking so that the project management team (and even the organisation) know that the project is being run well. That's no different in principle to a board of directors having an audit team who check things out for them and a financial audit team doing checks and reporting back to the finance director.

Unless the Project Manager is a devious and disreputable soul – so definitely not you then – she has nothing to fear from project audit, and actually the reverse. The Project Manager should be really pleased when project audit people appear in her office to do some checks. To draw a simple parallel, have you ever had a really tricky piece of work to do, and when you were finished you weren't too sure of it? Perhaps you asked an experienced colleague to cast an eye over the work for you. She did so and asked one or two questions. One question highlighted a mistake in your work, so you put it right. Then your colleague said, 'Well, other than that, it looks absolutely fine.' How did you feel then? Relieved? Grateful? Almost certainly both, and then you can add 'more confident' into the mix. Good project audit is like that and not to be confused with trouble-seeking nit-pickers whom you definitely don't want in the project audit role.

Project administration

If your project is of any size, it usually makes sense to have a *project administrator*. In large organisations, senior staff often have a personal assistant who manages the diary, books travel and accommodation, answers the phone, takes messages, sorts email, answers basic enquiries, writes letters . . . well, you know the sort of stuff. Good personal assistants are invaluable and really earn their keep. So, too, in the project.

Project Managers can not only waste a lot of time doing admin, but also get distracted from running the project because they're too focused on admin stuff. It often makes sense, then, to have one or more than one project administrator who can do the admin work that's associated with all projects. Project administrators are normally of a lower grade than the Project Manager and so are cheaper for the project, but also, as very good administrators, they can probably do the work in half the time the Project Manager would take anyway.

Some organisations centralise project administration and have a project office that gives this support to all projects. That's great for economy of scale, for gaining experience and so doing things very well. Also, the project office can then offer help to smaller projects that can't justify their own full-time administrators.

Team leader

Unless your project only has a single team, in which case the Project Manager often runs it, every team has a *team leader*. The number you have depends, obviously enough, on the number of teams working on the project at any one time. Teams are often formed mostly from inside your own organisation, but you may have supplier teams on your project as well. The supplier teams may be from outside your own organisation but they're inside the project and, if you're controlling the work, you need to include them in the same controls and reporting as for internal teams.

Many Project Managers maintain contact with team leaders both individually and by having regular team leader meetings where everyone can hear about progress across the project.

The Project Manager can also use this meeting to collect information such as progress and time sheet information. The Project Manager can also push information out. Team leaders can go back and tell their team members so that information cascades. In bigger projects, that can be a very useful communication mechanism.

Team leaders often do low level detailed planning for their teams' work, but usually work with the Project Manager to help produce the plans at stage and even project level because they can provide valuable information on what work is needed in the project.

Team members

Team members are the people doing most of the work of the project, so they're arguably the most important people of all in the project. The rest is just management.

Deciding the structure

If you're a Project Manager, the upper part of the structure can be a difficult area because the people involved are probably senior to you. You can't easily tell your managers what they should do and instruct them in their duties. In management, it's traditional that the more senior people tell the more junior people what to do. If you're asked about the structure, then that's great. If you're not asked, then you may need to persuade, and the logic behind the project organisation here may help. One thing's for sure: if your project management team or steering committee doesn't function well, it will be a significant problem in the project, and the Project Manager will have to do much more than is fair or reasonable.

Looking at the Organisation

With increasing frequency, projects today involve and affect many functional areas within an organisation. As a result, staff from these different areas must work together to successfully accomplish the project work. The *matrix organi-sation structure* works in two dimensions where staff belong in business units for management purposes but are then allocated to projects for their actual work.

Some organisations, and not least some UK government departments, like Matrix Management because staff time can be allocated in smaller units so staff are 'fully utilised'. That looks really good from a senior management perspective, but it can be a smokescreen because of the big difference between allocation and achievement. If staff are constantly flitting from one project to another – an hour here, two hours there – how committed and motivated are they going to be? Someone may be fully allocated but it doesn't mean she's fully productive. Staff who are permanently on a team, who identify with the project and who are committed to each other and to the success of the project are going to perform much better than staff who are flitting between projects. It may be that full-time project staff who spend 20 per cent of their time playing computer games while they're waiting for the next job to come up are more productive than staff who are 'fully utilised'. To read more on this, take a look at the book *Peopleware* by Tom DeMarco and Timothy Lister (Dorset House Publishing Company). The authors calculate that well-motivated staff in good organisations work 11 times faster than staff in poor organisations doing similar work. In the light of statistics like that, full utilisation seems rather less significant, and motivation and performance seem rather more important.

As Figure10-3 illustrates, in a matrix organisation structure, how people from different areas of the organisation are assigned to lead or work on projects. In Matrix Management, Project Managers guide the performance of project activities, while people's direct supervisors (from groups such as finance, manufacturing and sales, as in Figure 10-3) perform administrative tasks like formally appraising people's performance and approving promotions, salary increases or requests for leave. Because an individual can be on a project for less than 100 per cent of his time, she may work on more than one project at a time.

Shaded squares show staff allocation to projects

Figure 10-3: The general matrix organisation structure.

A matrix environment is classified as *weak, strong* or *balanced,* depending on the amount of authority the Project Managers have over their teams. So you get the full picture, here's a little more about each of these classifications:

✔ **Weak matrix:** Project team members receive most of their direction from their functional managers. Project Managers have little direct authority over team members and actually function more like project coordinators.

✔ **Strong matrix:** Companies with strong matrix structures choose Project Managers for new projects from a pool of people whose only job is to manage projects. The companies never ask these people to serve as team members. Often, these Project Managers form a single organisational unit that has its own head of department. In addition to directing and guiding project work, these Project Managers have certain administrative authority over the team members, such as the right to participate in their performance appraisals.

✔ **Balanced matrix:** This type of matrix environment is a blend of the weak and strong environments. People are assigned to run projects or serve as team members based on the projects' needs rather than on their job descriptions. Although the Project Manager may have some administrative authority over team members (such as approving leave requests), in general the Project Manager guides, coordinates and facilitates the project.

Advantages of the matrix structure

A matrix environment offers many benefits:

✓ Teams can assemble rapidly. Because you have a larger resource pool from which to choose your team, you may not have to wait as long for a skill to be available.

✓ Specialised expertise can be available for several different projects.

Disadvantages of the matrix structure

A matrix environment introduces a number of challenges which the Project Manager must successfully address. For example, team members:

✓ Are accountable to multiple managers who often have conflicting priorities

✓ May not be as familiar with each team's way of working

✓ May not be as committed to or productive in any one project, because they're constantly moving around

✓ May focus more on individual than project goals

Working successfully in a matrix environment

To be successful in a matrix environment, you need to coordinate the people allocated to your project, deflecting any forces that pull them in different directions. This section can help you, as a Project Manager, to get the highest-quality work from team members in a matrix environment, along with timely and effective support from the functional managers.

Team in this context means all the people working to build the project's products. In practice, you may have a number of teams, each with a team leader, so your work here is to get cohesion both across the project and within individual teams.

To get a project 'feel' and identity, and then to encourage team members to function well:

- Clarify the project vision and working relationships.

- Make it clear how the group(s) will work, and communicate so people aren't working across each other.

- Clarify each person's authority and how the project organisation fits together.

- Be aware of and attend to how people are functioning.

- Be sure everyone appreciates that they are important, no matter how junior. Adopt the maxim 'we, not me'.

- Build commitment by forging close links between the team members and the goal, and making sure everyone knows the significance of the work they are doing.

- Recognise good performance and actions which help the team. Just expressing appreciation has a huge impact.

In Matrix Management you also need functional managers on side to release staff resource. This is primarily the responsibility of the project management team or steering committee, but in practice you need to keep a close eye on it to build good relationships. You need to:

- Ask for functional managers' support. In some projects, support isn't forthcoming because it was never asked for in the first place.

- Head off problems in advance, such as agreeing how work conflicts will be resolved before you get to the point where you have work conflicts.

- Plan in sufficient detail so that you can tell functional managers what resource you need and when, and you don't understate it.

- Encourage your steering committee or project management team to maintain strong links with top management. A functional manager may be more willing to release staff if the CEO appreciates that some departmental targets may not be met because of heavy staff involvement in a business-critical project that's vital for the future of the whole organisation.

Chapter 11

Working With Teams and Specialists

*P*rojects usually involve working with people with different skill sets, from different areas within the organisation and possibly from outside it and who are used to working in different ways. Just to make it more fun, your project probably has a tight time schedule, so you'll need to move fast, and of course you need to get it pretty much right first time. No pressure then.

If you're working in a medium to large project, then as a Project Manager you'll probably be dealing with Team Leaders who in turn directly manage the teams. This can obviously make your work easier, but it can also make it harder because you need to be careful to provide encouragement and support but not tread on toes and bypass your Team Leaders.

Success in this kind of environment needs agreement on how to work to maximise contributions and minimise wasted time and mistakes. This chapter explains how to distinguish between the different degrees of involvement, make key assignments, encourage people to give their best and keep their commitments to the plan, and present an overall picture of team members' roles and responsibilities.

Working With Others

Unless your project is very small indeed and only needs you, you're going to need other people to help get the job done.

Treading carefully

It's probably not necessary to point out that good management relationships in a project are vital – but there, it's said anyway. As a manager, you need to tread a careful path to get and keep people on side without being overbearing or lax to the point that the job doesn't get done. It's easier if you know the people already but the chances are that some of the people in the project will be new to you, and you to them.

Balancing the communications

In managing the project, you need a balance in your communications. On the one hand, if you start explaining the obvious to Team Leaders, then they're going to get annoyed and feel that you don't trust them to get on and do the job that they're fully qualified and able to do. On the other hand, if you're not clear or detailed enough in your communication, you run the very real danger of misunderstanding, not getting what you wanted and then wasting time – and probably money – while people put things right.

Working with your own teams

Where people are allocated to you for the duration of the project then you have ultimate control and can direct their work easily. The Project Manager needs to develop a good relationship with the Team Leaders and work closely with them. At the end of the day though, both they and the Project Manager understand the authority structure in the project because it is inherent in the roles.

Working with occasional staff

Sometimes you will need to call on people to contribute who are only doing occasional work for the project. It may be a team or more likely individuals. The problem here is that they also have a 'day job' and many other things to deal with apart from the work for your project. Also the project won't normally have the immediacy and focus that comes with being on a more permanent project team.

The work of the organisational staff needs to be on the project plan and those staff made aware of the significance of their part. Clearly, just because a bit of work is small and of short duration doesn't mean that it is unimportant. Such small things can and do hold up a whole project if not done on time. Very experienced people such as lawyers are very well aware that their input is important. Less experienced people may need it gently explaining.

It's important to get commitment to the timely delivery of work, and in turn that means that for its part, the project should be clear on what it wants and give plenty of warning of when that work will be needed. The plan, then, is central to this control.

People who make promises and then fail to keep them create some of the worst frustrations in a project environment. Building in accountability is part of the delegation of the work.

When a person who doesn't report to you administratively promises to do something for you, holding him accountable can be a touchy issue. You may not try to hold him accountable, because you think it's inappropriate (after all, you're not his boss) or because you don't know how to do so. But remember: holding people accountable is appropriate and necessary when they've accepted a responsibility. You don't need authority to hold people accountable; the people just have to have accepted the responsibility.

Use the following approaches to hold people accountable when you don't have direct authority over them:

  ✔ **Find out who has direct authority over the person and bring that supervisor into the process.** Consider getting the approval of the person's boss when you ask the person to accept responsibility for a task. If a person's boss is unaware that his staff member agreed to perform a task for you, your chances of getting the boss's help if the person fails to perform as promised are small.

✔ **Put your agreement in writing.** Have you ever noticed how strangely people react when you put an informal agreement in writing? All of a sudden, they act as if you don't trust them. Don't let this reaction deter you. Put your agreement in writing to confirm it, to clarify the terms and to serve as a reminder to both you and the person agreeing to do the task.

✔ **Be specific.** The more clearly you make your request, the easier it is for the person to estimate the effort he needs to make to respond to the request and to produce the right result the first time. The Product Definitions in planning help enormously here (more in Chapter 5).

✔ **Follow up.** Discuss the schedule and how you will monitor the person's performance and to address any issues or questions that arise. If the person is new to projects and feels uneasy at being monitored, explain that this is normal in projects and necessary to keep things on track.

✔ **Get commitment.** When a person indicates that he'll help you out, be sure to get a firm, specific commitment that the desired result will be achieved by a specific time and for a specific cost. Beware of vague declarations like 'I'll give it my best effort' or 'You can count on me.'

✔ **Create a sense of urgency and importance.** You may want to minimise any pressure the person feels by offering to *understand* if he can't perform to your expectations because of one reason or another. Unfortunately, this approach can suggest that the work you're asking him to do isn't really that important, and actually increases the chance that he won't complete it. Instead, let the person know how his work influences other work on the project. Let him know why he needs to perform to expectations and what the consequences will be – to the project and the organisation – if he doesn't. The Work Flow Diagram can be really effective here as it shows clearly what else will be delayed – right through to the end of the project – if his product is delayed.

Working with suppliers

The third team area to consider is external suppliers. Remember that if you have teams working on your project but they're from outside your own organisation, they're nevertheless inside your project. The way that some UK organisations work with suppliers is more than worrying, and to read the way some agreements are set up, you'd be forgiven for thinking that the supplier is the enemy.

Supporting supplier teams

Some projects give very little help or support to supplier staff and then fast-forward to an aggressive position, invoking clauses in the contract if those staff don't do so well. Poor work from suppliers cannot be excused for a single moment, but a key point here is that supplier staff in the project need support too. To help hammer the point home, have a look at this quotation from the American space agency NASA's 'One Hundred Rules for NASA Project Managers':

> *In award fee situations, the government personnel should be making every effort possible to make sure the contractor gets a high score (i.e., be on schedule and produce good work). Contractors don't fail, NASA does and that is why one must be proactive in support.*

So, the supplier staff don't fail, you do. It's in your interest to help supplier staff as well as organisational staff, because if the suppliers succeed, you succeed. Obvious really, but you wouldn't think so when you see some projects.

Beware of accountants who don't understand projects and who assure you that it's okay to go with a cheap supplier because they'll protect the project with a 'penalty clause' in the contract. However, if you have such a clause, you'd better not need to invoke it because if you do, you just lost; you haven't got what you needed. You may get your money back, but if you wanted the money, you wouldn't have gone out for the supply in the first place. You wanted the project and now you haven't got it. So much for the penalty clause protecting the project then.

Choosing suppliers carefully

Given that if you need external supplier resource, your success will partly depend on those staff, it pays to choose your suppliers carefully. Suppliers need to make money to stay in business, so of course they must make a profit on the job. However, dangers occur when suppliers are concerned only about making a profit. This problem isn't unique to some large consultancy companies, but it's certainly very visible in them when their staff are focused on 'selling in' more days to their clients rather than on their client's project. Strangely, although smaller suppliers also need to watch their profit margins, they're often more focused on the client because each client is proportionately more important to them, rather than just being 'an account' – an item in a monthly sales target. You need suppliers who will work well on the project and integrate with other project staff.

Thinking time, not just costs

Suppose one supplier can do a job in three months for £100,000, and another can do the same job in two months for £200,000; which is actually the cheapest? Well, if your project is due to save £500,000 a month after it's finished, and using the second supplier means you'll get to the point of delivery a month earlier, the more expensive supplier is actually £400,000 cheaper. But that's only if you see the work in its full business context rather than in the narrow confines of the bid. If you use staff in your organisation who aren't used to setting up project contracts, you may need to sit them down and explain the bigger picture rather slowly!

Making Project Assignments

Effectively eliciting the help and support of others in the work you do is essential to get the most out of all team members. If you are involved in the project doing some of the technical work as well as project managing it all, then you need to take care. Think carefully about what you should do and what is best done by others. In that thinking, don't forget that you must allow a significant amount of your time to do the project management work. It is a major and common error to be so involved with the technical problems that you forget all about controlling the project . . . right up to the point that it fails.

Delving into delegation

The following sections help you decide what to delegate and to understand different degrees of delegation, and then how to support your delegations and achieve the best results possible.

✓ **Focus on things that you should do, not just like to do.** A common problem facing all managers, not just Project Managers, is that they don't leave their old jobs behind;

they still want to be *hands on.* That's okay if the person who's Project Manager is also taking a team role, but it's not okay if that involvement undermines the team members working on an activity. Neither is it okay if the Project Manager role gets neglected, causing the project to fail.

✔ **Recognise and accept that you may be able to do a job better.** Strangely perhaps, a problem in organisations is that people get promoted because they're very good! You may be frustrated to see team members not doing work as well as you could do it. Don't let that tempt you to try to do much more yourself.

✔ **Assign yourself to the tasks that you do best.** That applies to tasks such as project administration as well as to any technical work.

✔ **If possible, assign yourself to tasks that aren't on a project's critical path.** (See Chapter 6 for a discussion of critical paths.) When you have to stop working on a technical task that's on your project's critical path to deal with a project management problem, you immediately delay the entire project.

Understanding delegation of authority

Delegating authority, notably to Team Leaders, doesn't have to be an all-or-nothing proposition. Consider the following six degrees of delegation:

✔ **Get in the know.** Get the facts and bring them to me for further action.

✔ **Show me the way to go.** Develop alternative actions to take, based on the facts you've found, and then bring them to me along with the facts.

✔ **Go when I say so.** Prepare one or more of the actions proposed, but don't do anything until I confirm it's okay.

✔ **Go unless I say *no*.** Tell me what you propose to do and when, and take your recommended actions unless I tell you otherwise.

✔ **How'd it go?** Analyse the situation, develop a course of action, take action and let me know the results.

✔ **Just go!** Here's a situation; deal with it.

Delegating to achieve results

Delegation always involves some risk. However, you can take steps to improve the chances for successful performance:

1. **Clarify what you want to delegate.**

   Clearly describe the work. Specify what you want the other person to do and the results you require. If necessary, also explain what you *don't* want.

2. **Choose the right person.**

   Determine the skills and knowledge you feel a person must have to perform the task successfully, and don't delegate the task to a person who lacks them.

3. **Make the delegation correctly.**

   Explain the work, the expected effort and specify the date he should have the activity completed. Put this information in writing for clarity and future reference.

4. **Be available to answer questions.**

   Maintaining contact to resolve any ambiguities and unexpected situations. It also conveys to the person that the task is important to you.

5. **Monitor performance.**

   Set up frequent well-defined points at which you can monitor performance. Then keep to that schedule.

6. **Promptly address problems that arise.**

   If you feel the person's performance isn't satisfactory, discuss your concerns and develop steps to bring it back on track.

Chapter 12

Being an Effective Leader

In This Chapter

▶ Being a leader as well as a manager

▶ Knowing what makes for a good manager, and a bad one

▶ Understanding motivation and demotivation

▶ Seeing why conflict can be really beneficial

▶ Knowing how your teams are really doing, not just reading reports

*A*fter intense work on a tight schedule, you submit your Project Charter (the document that defines the project and includes all the plans see Chapter 2) for review and approval. A few days later, your boss comes to you and says:

> 'I have some good news and some bad news. Which would you like to hear first?'

> 'Tell me the good news,' you respond.

> 'Your charter's been approved.'

> 'So, what's the bad news?' you ask.

> 'Now you have to do the project!'

Suddenly, everything flashes from two dimensions to three and gets very real. Now you're working with others and your success from this point on will depend on their success! You move from being just a planner to a leader.

This chapter gives you some ideas about leadership in the context of a project and how to get the best out of your team. Doing so isn't just selfish either. Yes, good leadership helps you get your project delivered successfully, but if you do it right, then you also make team members' work enjoyable and allow them to develop and achieve.

Practising Leadership

Managing is mostly concerned with controlling the work of others and yourself, but *leadership* involves being in front and inspiring others, not just throwing work at them.

Make no mistake: if you're a Project Manager, leadership is a vital part of your role. You can plan well, but if the teams don't work well, then you're going to have problems.

The good news is that team members (with a few exceptions) want to do a good job, so you will be working with them, not against them. You know yourself that you are the most satisfied when you have achieved something and done it very well. Your team members feel the same, and there lies one of the keys to effective project management: your team members are like you. Too many people go through a strange metamorphosis when they're appointed to a management position, a bit like Jekyll and Hyde or Harry Enfield's sketch of Kevin's 13th birthday when he turns into a teenager. Then they think that staff should be treated very differently to how they liked to be managed when they were in that position.

Understanding what makes a good leader

To be effective yourself, it helps to stand back a bit and analyse what makes someone a good leader and manager, and also what makes for a bad one. Although this section goes on to spell out the factors, you probably already know most if not all of them from your own experience of being managed.

So, think back to those who've managed you. Who did you like working for? Who managed you so that you could give your very best, and what were the characteristics of their management styles? Then think about managers who weren't so good, who closed you down and made life difficult. What was it about those poor managers that made them poor?

A few characteristics are set out in the nearby sidebar 'Management characteristics', but you can add more. Faces will probably come to mind as you consider each characteristic.

Management characteristics

Good managers:

✔ Are cool headed and rational when problems crop up

✔ Are supportive and available

✔ Give opportunities and challenges

✔ Have a clear sense of direction and communicate objectives well

✔ Have a sense of proportion so minor problems aren't treated as crises

✔ Plan well so their staff aren't forever racing to meet unrealistic deadlines

✔ Recognise and show appreciation of good work and extra effort

✔ Respect their staff

✔ Trust and give responsibility

✔ Value the views of the staff, even if the manager finally disagrees sometimes

Bad managers:

✔ Are control freaks and micromanagers

✔ Are emotional, including regularly getting angry and having emotional highs and lows

✔ Are power hungry and play power games

✔ Don't listen to their staff

✔ Focus on the task only – at the expense of the staff

✔ Find fault and apportion blame if things go wrong, and even if they don't

✔ Take all the credit for achievements

'How do I become a good manager?' you might ask. On one level the answer's easy. You emulate the things that you've seen in good managers and avoid the things that you've seen in bad managers. You know the things that helped you give your best, and when you really wanted to do that because you enjoyed what you did, and you also know the sorts of things that closed you down and made you want to give up and go home early.

Leading in the hard times too

Some people think that leadership is great and people will follow if you're going somewhere nice and the journey there will be pleasant. That's not true, however, and leaders can inspire people to follow them and endure even hardship. One of the best examples has to be Winston Churchill, who on being appointed Prime Minister in a time of war said to the House of Commons: 'I would say to the House, as I said to those who have joined the Government: I have nothing to offer but blood, toil, tears and sweat.' Churchill was an inspiring leader, and although not many people are gifted to that extent, you can provide good leadership on tough tasks.

Leading older, more senior team members

It can be difficult to lead if team members are senior to you in experience and also in age. It may help to remember that projects are all about roles. Your role is to manage. That doesn't mean that you're inferior or superior to any team member, just that your role is different. Chapter 11 is all about project roles and their significance.

Developing personal power

To get a job done you need authority, and it will help you in the project if you think through just where that authority comes from.

The very title *Project Manager* gives authority and everyone knows that the Project Manager has day-to-day responsibility for the project. A natural respect and compliance follows from Team Leaders and team members who can see from the project organisation structure, even if they haven't already realised, that they're accountable to you. Unless you give the teams reason to challenge that inbuilt authority, then you can expect it to stand.

As the captain of the ship (see Chapter 11 on project organisation), you have initial authority on two grounds:

- **Appointment:** Unless your project is very small and in your own area of work, more senior managers will have appointed you to the role of Project Manager. That appointment itself displays their confidence in you and reflects an authority within the organisation.

- **Delegation:** This project is being run for the organisation, not your own ends, and was commissioned by a sponsor or perhaps even a more senior group such as a management board. You're running the project on behalf of those who commissioned it, and therefore you have their authority, not just your own.

Both of these grounds add to your confidence in your position because you're backed by authority that is higher than your current position. That point should help too when you come to manage more senior people who are working on your project.

Knowing What Motivates

To have a healthy project that stays on schedule, you need motivated staff who will work well in terms of the quantity of work they do in a given period and the quality of it. Remember, if the quality is poor, that affects the project schedule as well as the end product, because of all the correction and re-testing. So what makes for good motivation on teams and within the project as a whole?

Learning from Fred Herzberg

There have been many books and theories on motivation over the years, but one of the simplest and most powerful models is from Fred Herzberg (1923–2000), an American psychologist who became a leading light in management practice. Fred Herzberg's model is great for management, and is highly relevant for creating productive project teams.

Herzberg says that people will normally give an average performance – something he calls *the potter line*, where people potter along doing what they think is a fair day's work for a fair day's pay. Things like money, good working conditions and company cars, he argues, won't motivate people to give more than an average performance.

You may know yourself, if you have a company car for example, that when you first got it you were delighted. But very quickly it became part of your normal environment and now you jump into the car and rarely think about when you didn't have it. Fred Herzberg called things like fair pay, good working conditions and company benefits *hygiene factors*.

Where Herzberg differs from many management experts is where he says you can't neglect these hygiene factors or you drag performance down below the potter line. You need to have good working conditions for your teams, so fight hard to get them if you need to. Try to make sure that team members are paid properly for the work they do. However, important though these things are, they don't motivate.

Herzberg argues that the *motivators* are things like achievement, recognition, doing sensible and worthwhile work, having responsibility, moving on in a career with promotion, and having opportunity for personal growth. It's those things that make people, including you, perform above the potter line.

Clearly, then, if you want good team performance you need to build opportunities for achievement and personal growth into the way that you allocate your project work. If you always give someone boring, meaningless work that provides no interest or challenge, don't be surprised if your project performance indicators show that person pottering along and not having the drive and productivity you're really looking for. If she's paid poorly and sitting on a broken chair in a drab, beaten-up office as well, then you can confidently look forward to productivity well below the potter line.

Understanding demotivation

The causes of demotivation have also been identified with a useful demotivation model. The model has the three elements of putting in the effort, seeing the result and then getting recognition and reward

A break between any of those three components leads to demotivation, as shown in Figure 12-1.

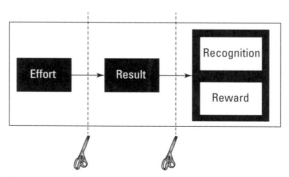

Figure 12-1: Demotivation model – source unknown.

Working hard but not seeing a result is demotivating. Taking the opposite perspective, a research scientist who keeps on experimenting but doesn't see any result for some years has to be very highly motivated to keep going. Or, someone puts in the effort, sees the result and then . . . nothing. Nobody notices and nobody offers any reward for all of that effort – that's demotivating and is highly likely to affect performance adversely on future tasks.

As a Project Manager you can do something about both break points and so do much to avoid demotivation. First, considering Herzberg's point in the last section about meaningful work, try to design tasks on your project so that team members see an end result. Then, when that result is forthcoming, give recognition and, if it's within your power, reward. You can at least recognise achievements, even if you can't influence reward. The earlier sidebar 'Management characteristics' listed recognising and showing appreciation of work and extra effort as attributes of a good manager.

Developing Your Teams

Merely assigning people to tasks doesn't create a project team. A *team* is a collection of people who are committed to common goals and who depend on one another to do their jobs. Project teams consist of members who can and must make a valuable and unique contribution to the project.

Just how much involvement you will have in creating effective teams depends on the nature and particularly the size of your project. If you're in a large project, you will have Team Leaders who are primarily responsible for the teambuilding aspects. However, even then, you have a role in establishing a project identity and encouraging Team Leaders in their teambuilding work. You may even get involved in assisting with the teambuilding such as by going along to give project briefings. If you do have Team Leaders, your leadership role must tread the normal careful path in management of being supportive and engaged on the one hand but not interfering or undermining Team Leader authority on the other. In a smaller project, you may be running the team, and in that case the teambuilding work falls entirely to you.

A team is different from other associations of people who work together. For example:

- A *group* consists of people who work individually to accomplish their particular assignments on a common task.

- A *committee* consists of people who come together to review and critique issues, propose recommendations for action and, on occasion, implement those recommendations.

Defining operating processes

Develop the procedures that you and your teams will use to support the day-to-day work. Having these procedures in place allows people to effectively and efficiently perform their tasks, and to know how to communicate. In turn, that clarity will help avoid misunderstanding and conflict and will contribute to a positive atmosphere in the project. At a minimum, develop procedures for the following:

- **Communication:** These processes involve sharing project-related information in writing and verbally. Communication procedures may include:

    - How to address special issues that arise, such as on technical matters involved with the development

    - How to set up regularly scheduled reports and meetings to record and review progress, warn of problems and newly identified risks, and communicate suggestions and ideas

    - When and how to document informal discussions

    - When and how to use email

    - Which types of information should be in writing, and what can be reported or discussed verbally

- **Conflict resolution:** These processes involve resolving differences of opinion between teams regarding project work. You can develop the following conflict-resolution procedures:

    - *Standard approaches* (normal steps that teams take to find a solution)

    - *Escalation procedures* (steps to take if the people involved can't readily resolve their differences)

✔ **Decision making:** Develop guidelines for choosing the most appropriate approach for a situation, including consensus and decision by technical expert. Also develop escalation procedures – the steps you take when the normal decision-making approaches get bogged down.

 Think long and very hard to keep written information to the minimum. Written communications all contribute to project overheads and also sap your team members' energies if they're forever having to complete project documentation instead of getting on with the job. Turn to Chapter 14 for more on the whole area of project communications.

 Government figures in 2010 showed that UK police officers spent, on average, 20 per cent of their time filling in forms and only 14 per cent actually out on patrol, their key front-line activity. Be careful and monitor how much of your own time and that of your project staff is consumed in project overheads rather than in delivering the project's products.

Helping your teams function

When team members trust each other, have confidence in each other's abilities, can count on each other's promises and communicate openly, they can devote all their efforts to performing their project work instead of spending time dealing with interpersonal frustrations. One approach is to guide them through the following commonly used phases:

✔ **Forming:** This phase involves meeting team members and discussing project objectives, work assignments and so forth. Share the Project Plan, introduce people to each other, and discuss each person's background, responsibilities and areas of expertise. Forming is something you may want to do project-wide, not just within each team.

✔ **Storming:** This stage involves raising and resolving personal conflicts about the project or other team members. As part of the storming stage, do the following:

• Encourage people to discuss any concerns they have about the Project Plan's feasibility, and be sure you address those concerns.

• Encourage people to discuss any reservations they may have. For example, a junior and inexperienced team member may feel nervous being surrounded by highly qualified specialists.

- Focus these discussions on ways to ensure successful task performance.

You can initially speak privately with people about issues if they're uncomfortable about bringing them up in front of the entire team. Eventually, though, you must discuss their concerns with the entire team to achieve a sense of mutual honesty and trust.

✔ **Norming:** This stage involves developing the standards and operating guidelines that govern team members' behaviour. Encourage members to establish these team norms instead of relying on the procedures and practices they use in their normal functional areas. Examples of these norms include the following:

  - **How people present and discuss different points of view:** Some people present points of view politely to the point of understating them, and others enthusiastically debate things to the point of appearing aggressive as they work to resolve points.

  - **Participation in meetings:** Some people sit back and observe, and others actively participate and share their ideas. The norm will be to encourage active participation.

  - **Timeliness of meeting attendance:** Some people always show up for meetings on time, but others are habitually 15 minutes late. Set the norm for this project, which of course will normally be that people show up on time, or everyone's time is wasted.

✔ **Performing:** This stage involves doing project work, monitoring schedules and budgets, making necessary changes and keeping people informed.

Teams won't automatically pass through these stages; they have to be guided.

As the Project Manager, you will need to periodically assess how the teams feel they're performing. Again, if you're working with Team Leaders then you may want to do this mostly through them by checking things out at a Team Leaders' meeting. But nothing is as good as a first-hand view, so schedule time to go and see how each team is getting on – adopt the MBWA style, which is *management by walking about*. You don't have to say much except to encourage and show interest, but you can observe. Here are a few pointers:

- Are the team members upbeat and cheerful, or are they downcast and gloomy?

- Do the team members show an active interest in the work when you ask them about it, or are there signs of disengagement and just 'going through the motions'?

- Are they working together, or is everyone isolated and working on their own, even where they are supposed to be building products together?

- Is the work area organised and tidy, or cluttered and disorganised?

- How do team members seem to relate to the Team Leader? Is it happily as a colleague or are there signs of reluctant obedience or even disrespect? For example, if you see the Team Leader speak to a team member, perhaps to ask something, what does the team member do when the Team Leader turns away? (Watch out of the corner of your eye – don't look directly.) Does the team member simply get on with the work, or does she look across at another team member and raise her eyes to the sky?

Harnessing conflict

It's a common mistake to think of conflict as always being something bad. If conflict is destructive, then certainly it's negative, but positive conflict also exists. *Positive conflict* is where two team members disagree and fight it out, but both thoroughly respect the other's view, and often both have great fun arguing the point through. This sort of conflict drives analysis deep, and when the outcome is finally agreed, both team members are fully confident in it.

Strangely, people who get on together too easily, who tend to see things the same way or who cave in at the first hint of an opposing view can end up with a superficial result that hasn't been properly thought through or challenged. However, the conflict is time consuming, so who you put on a task depends on the importance of that task, how soon you want it finished, and how important it is for the outcome to be right. A critical design product may justify putting staff on to the work who are going to see things differently and who are strong characters; they'll go deep. Deciding in which order to paint the three inner walls of the stationery cupboard probably doesn't justify too much in the way of conflict and deep discussion. So, yet another dimension for your resource planning – there's a lot to project management, isn't there?

If you don't have team members who see things differently, you can engineer the situation by getting one to deliberately attack a product, such as a design, to see whether the other person can counter the arguments. Or you can get everyone to take on the negative stance to try to spot the problems with an idea or a design product. For more on the negative stance, you might like to read about the *black hat* thinking style in Edward de Bono's book *Six Thinking Hats*, published by Penguin, or check out Edward de Bono's website for a short explanation.

Stoking the Boilers

A final word about leadership and motivation is a reminder to keep your teams well motivated and encouraged throughout the project. Getting your team members to appreciate your project's value and feasibility helps you build initial enthusiasm. However, if the project lasts longer than a couple of weeks, the team's initial momentum can die without continual reinforcement from you. In general, people working on a particular task need to know how they're doing over time for three reasons:

- ✔ Achieving intermediate milestones provides personal and group satisfaction.

- ✔ Recognising their successes confirms to people that they're on the right track and motivates them.

- ✔ Successfully completing intermediate steps reinforces people's belief that they can accomplish the final goals.

Part IV
Steering the Project to Success

'We thought by giving you a special uniform to wear as project manager, Ponsonby, would give you more authority with your team.'

In this part . . .

*I*t's one thing planning out a project and printing it off in full colour for everyone to admire. It's quite another when the project starts and things begin to go a little differently, where other people get involved and somebody decides they want a change . . . or two.

Project control is essential to keep the project on track and heading towards successful delivery. This part covers ways of monitoring progress and keeping in control, dealing with change and the vital area of communications – keeping information flowing through the project – and then bringing the project to an orderly close. It also takes a quick look at technology and software that can be a big help.

Chapter 13

Tracking Progress and Staying in Control

· ·

In This Chapter

▶ Monitoring progress against the plan

▶ Checking up on spending against the plan

▶ Making corrections to keep on track

▶ Controlling change

· ·

*H*aving planned your project and started it off, you now need to keep your eye on the ball and keep it on track. All projects experience problems, but far too many Project Managers don't detect that things are off the plan until the deviation is severe. At that point it's much harder, and sometimes impossible, to put right. It's a bit like walking across some open moorland. If you go a couple of degrees off course and you detect this quickly, you need take only a few steps to get back on track. If you don't find out for several hours that you deviated by two degrees . . . well, you get the picture. When you run your project, you can be very sure of one thing: it won't go exactly to plan. That makes it all the more important to identify deviations from the plan promptly so that you can react quickly and make the necessary corrections.

In this chapter, then, look forward to see how you can track progress quickly and effectively, and look at your options when things don't quite go to plan. You can also expect some very real help in controlling change in the project and avoiding that common project killer, scope creep. If you put into practice what you read in this chapter, you may not eliminate scope creep, but you'll certainly go a long way towards it.

Understanding Progress Control

There are three key underpinning elements for effective progress control. Those key things are having a good plan, having clear and frequent milestones and then putting in place an effective progress-reporting mechanism.

Having a reliable plan

Knowing that projects just about always go off track could lead the less well informed to think that it's not worth spending much time on planning. Actually the opposite is true. The fact that the project is going to go off plan means that the plan is even more important..

When a large ship sets out on a voyage, it has a sail plan that shows the planned course to the destination port. However, this course is the one route the ship is guaranteed not to follow. Winds and water currents will push the ship off course. However, the planned course is all the more important because that's what the ship will constantly correct to in order to ensure that it arrives safely at its destination.

You need a plan, then, but if the plan itself is unrealistic, incomplete and superficial, then clearly it's going to be next to useless for control. The plan isn't just some luxury that, in an ideal world, projects really should have if they have the time to create them: It is essential for effective control.

The plan must also be up to date, within a few days at least. If something is reported as off track, then you need to be able to assess the impact and work out your options. If you last updated the plan seven weeks ago, it isn't going to be a lot of help in planning where to go from here, because you won't know where 'here' is. Get into the discipline of updating your plan once a week with 'actuals' of what has been delivered, the timings of those deliveries and what resource, including staff time, has been expended.

Having frequent milestones

To know for sure where you are, you need milestones.. The deliverables or products in each stage form natural milestones and so provide an excellent foundation for progress control. Chapter 5, on product-based planning, advises you to have 15–30 defined products for project, broken down into more detail in the Stage Plans to give 15–30 at the stage level of detail. The importance of having frequent milestones becomes increasingly clear as you read on in this chapter.

Where you are using a computer-based project management tool to maintain the plan, it will track progress on the Gantt Chart using *percentage complete* for each activity. The percentage complete is shown with the solid bar in the middle of the activity bar filling up like a thermometer. The approach has drawbacks but you can find more on it later in the chapter.

Using a reporting mechanism

Clearly, you aren't going to have good progress control without an effective reporting mechanism accompanying it to show you when the project reaches milestones. If you aren't using products, despite the approach in this book, then you'll need regular estimates of progress from those doing the work. If you use products as milestones, then you need a mechanism to flag up when products have been delivered.

A product is *complete* when it's been quality checked and signed off. If it hasn't passed test yet, it isn't complete.

Harnessing Product Power

The progress-tracking mechanism of percentage complete on activities does have some problems. The mechanism is known to be unreliable because at best it's based on an estimate and at worst team members exaggerate the progress they've made. Using products as a progress measure avoids the problems of estimation for progress reports. With products, progress isn't a matter of estimation but a matter of factual reporting. Which products are complete (quality checked and signed off) and which aren't? That gives you – and the project sponsor or steering committee – an accurate statement of exactly where you are in the stage and the project.

Compiling a Work Checklist

A *Work Checklist* is an extraordinarily simple device, but a very powerful one. It's just a list of products to be produced in a stage, together with the products' target delivery dates and then, when they are complete, their actual delivery dates. You can also add a column for the variance between the two. Table 14-1 gives an example.

Table 14-1	The Work Checklist		
	Work Checklist – Stage 6 – Position at 7 July		
Product	*Target Delivery*	*Actual Delivery*	*Days +/–*
Inner gears	12 June	15 June	–3
Power and fuse housing	20 June	20 June	0
Feeder tubes	3 July	3 July	0
Control panel	8 July	6 July	+2
Conveyor mechanism	12 July		
Assembled rotor unit	20 July		

Even if, surprisingly, you don't have intimate engineering knowledge of inner gears or rotor units, you can nevertheless see at a glance where this stage is. The checklist shows clearly what has been delivered, when, and how the date compares with that on the plan. Remember, a completed product is one that has been quality checked and signed off, so with the Work Checklist you know that products have been confirmed as meeting their specified quality requirements; they have not been thrown together and finished in a hurry.

Most experienced Project Managers agree that the first sign of trouble on a project isn't overspending, as many assume, but rather slippage on delivery. In the context of delivery, the Work Checklist gives even more value as a monitoring tool.

Getting visual

Chapter 5 on product planning shows how to create a Work Flow Diagram. You can use this diagram in all sorts of ways in the project, but it's relevant here because you can adapt it to form a very simple and highly visual progress report.

Now you've seen the Work Checklist and the progress-annotated Work Flow Diagram, you can fully understand why frequent milestones are a great idea and why all products should be milestones. It isn't onerous jotting down the date of delivery of a product and altering the colour of its symbol on the Work Flow, and in return you have extraordinarily precise progress-tracking information based on factual reporting of products states (not-complete or complete), not on someone's guess of percentage complete on an activity.

Monitoring at different levels

Monitoring and reporting progress is often at stage level. However, sometimes project sponsors, steering committee members and others in the organisation such as a management board like to see project-level progress – the big picture. That's no problem, and you can colour-code the Work Flow Diagram (see the previous section) in the project-level plan as well as the stage-level diagrams.

Equally, if a team is working on a complex *Work Package* – a work assignment to build a product or a group of related products – the Team Manager may well have drawn up a more detailed plan. This lower level plan will include a Work Flow Diagram at a more detailed level still than the stage-level plan. If there is a lower-level Work Flow Diagram, this too can be used for progress monitoring where the Project Manager is keeping tabs on the progress of individual Work Packages.

Taking Action When Off Track

And yes, the word *when* and not *if* appears in the title of this section. Projects are always going into the unknown to some extent, and you can almost guarantee that your project won't go exactly the way you thought. If your project doesn't go exactly to plan, don't panic: that's normal. You need to:

1. **Find out why the project is off track.**

2. **Look at all the things you could do.**

3. **Decide which action or actions you're going to take.**

4. **Take the action you have decided on.**

5. **Monitor to see whether the actions are working. If the steps are not working, go back to step 1 to find out why, and follow the other steps through again.**

The rest of this section explores these steps in more detail.

In a panic, Project Managers often leave out the first two steps and jump into step 3, but that's a big mistake. It's all too easy to rush into an action when actually that action isn't the easiest, cheapest or most effective. Knee-jerk reactions are rarely the best ones when dealing with project problems.

Finding out why

When you hit a problem, first look for the underlying causes and try to understand the characteristics of the problem. This may well involve talking to a Team Leader or two and perhaps some team members and external supplier specialists. In the case of a problem affecting the overall running of the project, perhaps it would be good to have an informal chat with the sponsor or one or two members of the project steering committee as well. It's only when you properly understand both the characteristics and the causes of deviations from the plan that you can come up with sensible corrective actions. Ask the following questions:

- ✔ Is the project off track or is the project is 'right' but the plan is unrealistic? You may need to adjust the plans for the rest of the project in the light of this experience.

- ✔ Is this a problem with planned work, or has extra necessary work been discovered that wasn't anticipated on the plan?

- ✔ Is there a problem because the work requires more effort than expected, or is it that the team members haven't been able to put in the planned time?

✔ Are the team members going more slowly than expected because of unfamiliarity and inexperience? Would it help to ask for more experienced staff, or would the learning curve of new staff getting to understand the project only make things worse still?

✔ Have the teams been held up because necessary equipment isn't available? For example, delays in other projects have held up the release of equipment.

✔ Is the problem because something is more complicated than anticipated? Does that mean that other products will also be more complicated?

✔ Is this problem a one-off problem that affects only this part of the work? Or is everything is going to take longer than expected?

✔ Is the cause of the problem something you can control or is it, by its very nature, outside your control, such as higher than normal sickness levels due to a particularly nasty bug circulating?

✔ Is the activity on a critical path? Delayed activities on a critical path will delay your overall project schedule (see Chapter 6 for a detailed discussion of critical paths). If the activity is on the critical path, you'll need to take more extensive control action than if it has spare time that can absorb some or all of the delay.

✔ Is the activity on a path that's close to being critical? Activities on non-critical paths can have some delays before their paths become critical..

✔ Has the work already been identified as involving risk? If so, have you got some management actions planned already and set down in your Risk Register? (See Chapter 9 for more on the Risk Register.)

✔ Have you already encountered problems with this activity? Unless new factors have arisen, the recurring problem suggests that previous control actions aren't proving adequate.

Thinking about what to do

It's important to 'think wide' when considering possible actions to get a project back on track. A common knee-jerk reaction is to throw more staff resource or money at the problem, but that isn't always the best thing to do. Indeed, for some problems putting more people onto the work just makes matters worse.

A great help is to bring in the team leader and possibly team members to talk about the problem. It's often the case that team members themselves can see solutions, especially if they're technical experts and have 'been there, done it and got the t-shirt'.

When considering your options for bringing the project back on track, include the following in your thinking:

- ✔ **Use contingency to absorb an overrun if the activity has no float.** If the activity is something that you can't put extra people on, just accept the fact – it's what contingency is there for. However, if you're unhappy that it's taken up too much of your contingency for this point in the project, you may be able to buy back some contingency time by putting more staff on a later activity and so shortening its duration.

- ✔ **Split the work.** It may be that part of the work must be done now, and although it was preferable that the whole job was completed, in fact some of it can be done later in parallel with other things.

Deciding what you'll do

Having considered a range of options for action, now's the time to make your mind up on what action or actions you're going to take. Your decision is likely to hinge around three factors:

- ✔ What you think will be the most effective
- ✔ What the cost is likely to be in money and staff time
- ✔ What the impact on other project work will be

For the last of these factors, your plan needs to be up to date – repeating the important point from the earlier section 'Having a reliable plan'. Computer tools can really come into their own when looking at impacts, because you can do 'what if' projections using the tool.

Taking action

Having reached a decision on what to do, perhaps in consultation with the steering committee if the deviation is significant, you must now adjust your plans to include the actions. You will then adjust the work in line with the revised plans.

Monitoring the action

In some cases, after the control action is put into effect, that's the end of the matter. But in many cases you need to check whether your actions are proving effective. If the actions are working, that's all well and good, but if not, you'll need to look at why that is, see what range of actions are now possible in the light of this new information, choose what to do . . . Yes, go through all the steps again. Then monitor again. If the new actions aren't working too well either, then you go back around the steps for a third time.

Monitoring Work and Costs

Progress monitoring is very important to be sure that you deliver on time. However, progress isn't the only thing to watch. You also need to keep an eye on work effort and costs – which, of course, are related.

Keeping an eye on work effort

It may be that products are being delivered on time but are taking more work effort than expected. Comparing work effort expended with work effort planned can highlight when people are:

✔ Cutting corners on quality

✔ Encountering unexpected difficulties doing the work

✔ Incorrectly expanding or reducing the scope of an activity

✔ More or less qualified than anticipated

To monitor work effort, you need to collect data on the actual effort spent on each activity to build each product.

Good computer tools often produce time sheets at the click of an icon. If you use the computer to print out the time sheets, you make life easy for your team members who just need to fill in the remaining information each week. They'll be much more open to providing information for you if, in turn, you've made the reporting as easy as possible for them.

If you decide to use *per cent completed* alongside product delivery to monitor progress, because it's included in your software package, be careful. It's not a reliable way to indicate progress, and Chapter 5 explains why. For example, saying that your new product design is 30 per cent complete is virtually meaningless, because you can't determine objectively *how much* of the thinking and creating is actually done. Suggesting that you have completed 30 per cent of your design because because three of the ten days allotted for its performance have passed is equally incorrect. The first indicator is a measure of *resource* use, and the second is a measure of *time* elapsed. Neither measure indicates the amount of substantive *work* completed.

Monitoring expenditure

Alongside tracking progress, you must monitor your project's spending to verify that it's in line with the plans and, if it's not, to address any deviations. You may think that you can determine project funds used to date and funds remaining just by reading the balance in your project's financial account. However, if you're working in an organisation of any size, spending project funds usually involves several steps before an item is actually paid for. In particular you need to discriminate between money spent, money committed (an order has been placed but the bill hasn't been paid yet) and money not yet committed.

Tracking spending against the plan

To keep control of project spending, you need to compare the amounts it was planned to spend with the amounts that were actually spent. There's usually no need to get complicated about it, and you can set up a simple report format using a spreadsheet.

You may spend more or less money on your project activities than you planned, for the following reasons:

- ✔ You receive the bills for goods or services later than you planned, so they're paid for later than you planned.

- ✔ You buy and take delivery of items early, or just prepay, to receive special discounts or sale prices.

- ✔ You don't need certain goods or services that you budgeted for in your plan.

- ✔ You find you need goods or services that you didn't budget for in your plan.

Differentiating between overspending and early spending

Even if spending is greater than planned for this point, it may still not be a problem. An important check is whether the spending is overspending or something has been bought in advance of what was originally planned – the early purchasing mentioned in the second bullet point in the previous section. In the case of early spending, the stage (or project) will actually finish close to target, but in the case of overspending, then clearly it won't.

Automating your expenditure tracking

Before developing a way of monitoring the project's expenditures, first check the nature and capabilities of your organisation's financial tracking system. Most organisations have a financial system that maintains records of all expenditures. Often the system also maintains records of accounts payable. Unfortunately, many financial systems categorise expenses by cost centre but don't have the capacity to classify expenses by components within a project, and if that's true for your organisation, then you need to find something else to provide the additional detail you require.

Dealing with Change

Another important area of control in your project is change control. Look out, there's a project killer about, and its name is *scope creep*. Scope creep, as the name suggests, is a change to scope, but it's made up of small movements – and actually *small* is the problem.

The management writer Charles Handy uses an example of a frog in his book *The Age of Unreason* when discussing the effect of small changes in the market on companies. Please don't try this at home. If you drop a live frog into boiling water, it will jump out very smartly. If, however, you put a live frog into cold water and very slowly heat the water up, the frog will allow itself to be boiled to death. Apparently, frogs can't detect incremental changes in temperature.

Projects can, and do, suffer the same fate as the frog and the companies Charles Handy describes. Many small changes build up to represent a very big amount that the project can't absorb and which proves unmanageable and so fatal.

So what's the answer to scope creep? Simple: change control. Note the word *control*. We're not talking about change *prohibition*. In fact, prohibiting change in the project is usually damaging, but sometimes it's impossible anyway. The thing to try to eliminate isn't change but *uncontrolled* change.

You might think that you don't need change control because you don't want to allow changes at all. If so, consider correction of mistakes, compliance with new standards and taking on board good ideas that will improve the project.

This section helps you set up a change control process to manage change. It provides some helpful steps to follow when considering and acting on a change request.

Understanding types of change

Different types of change are significant because you may fund them in different ways. Where something has been delivered by a supplier and it's wrong, then it needs to be changed to be put right. If the original specification is clear, then the cost of this corrective change will fall to the supplier. But when the change is because the project customer has had a change of mind or something has changed in the business environment, then the cost of that change will fall to the customer. When additional work falls to an external supplier as a result, there will normally be an additional charge.

Setting up change procedures

To get a change, it has to be asked for, considered, approved (or not) and then implemented. By definition, if you want to avoid uncontrolled change, there needs to be control. You can do this very simply with the use of a Change Request form – but of course this can be electronic and sent by email, it doesn't have to be paper.

A *Change Request* should set down basic information, but that may be supplemented by the Project Manager after the request has been analysed. It should have basic information included on 'what' and 'why' as a minimum. In some cases, until some exploratory investigation has been done, it may not be possible to say exactly what's involved in making the change. Basic information includes:

- ✔ Name of the person asking for the change
- ✔ Date of the request
- ✔ Description, including impacts of making the change
- ✔ Reason for the change, including advantages, or saying if the change is mandatory

This information may be recorded in a Change Log and then supplemented with more information and the eventual decision on the change request.

- ✔ Work needed to effect the change
- ✔ Decision taken, to agree the change or refuse it
- ✔ Date the change request is closed

Having a *Change Log* is really helpful in the project, because it gives you an overview of the change requests received and what is happening to each. You can use a spreadsheet for your log and then you have the advantage that it can be sorted in different ways. For example, you may normally keep it so that live changes are at the top and closed change requests that have now been dealt with are sorted to the bottom.

Do bear in mind that you may need to consult other people about a particular change request, such as technical experts on teams, or the sponsor or steering committee members if it's something that requires authority beyond your own delegated authority, such as the change being high cost. Don't forget to allow for that time and involvement in your plans.

Budgeting for change

In the same way that you need to set aside some time in the project for dealing with changes, so too you're going to need some budget. If there's no change budget, then any change request will have to go to the sponsor because, by definition, it's not on the plan that the sponsor originally authorised.

How much there should be in a change budget depends on two main factors. The first is the amount of change anticipated in the project and the second is how much the sponsor wants to delegate decisions to the Project Manager.

The sponsor can set two dimensions on a change budget: a total amount and an item amount. So, for example, the Project Manager must go back to the sponsor if the total changes exceed a limit of £25,000 or for any single change that will cost £5,000 or more.

Looking at four control dogs

Some people, and many senior business managers, live in a comfortable, rose-tinted world where project changes can be absorbed with no impact. Sadly, projects happen in a real world with some very real change dynamics.

Different project approaches identify different control factors. The Project Management Institute (PMI) recognises four, and that's realistic. Nick Graham was teaching project management to a group of police officers, and came up with the analogy of four dogs (in their case, police dogs) pulling on a piece of project 'canvas'. As illustrated in Figure 13-1, the four dogs are cost, quality, scope and time.

The piece of project 'canvas' is very strong; it won't stretch and it won't tear. If one of the dogs pulls a corner of the canvas, something's got to give. Perhaps the canvas will pull sideways and just one other dog will get pulled along, or perhaps it will pull the other side and two dogs will get dragged, or perhaps all three will be taken in tow.

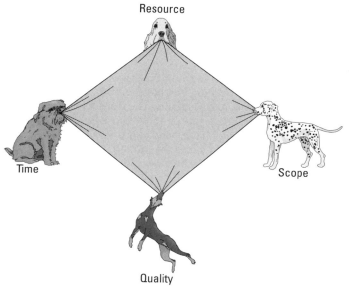

Figure 13-1: The four control dogs.

The dogs model is so simple you can keep it in your head when you're thinking about a change. If the 'scope' dog pulls the canvas, then what action is available to you as a Project Manager? You could ask for an increase in resource to deal with the change, but keep the quality the same and maintain the delivery date. Or perhaps you could ask for extra staff resource, but allow a bit more time as well so that the project can take a bit longer to accommodate the extra work.

Sometimes one of the control points is fixed, as in the case of the rather stout-looking 'Time' dog in Figure 13-1. This project must be delivered by the end of the financial year, and that's not up for debate. So, if there is to be a decrease in resource (the 'Resource' dog pulls), you have only two dogs left to consider. Should you reduce quality and do less testing, or leave something out, or both?

You may notice in Figure 13-1 that the 'Quality' dog looks a bit thin and weedy. It isn't fed on such good dog food as the other three dogs and is weaker. In many projects – not yours of course – the Quality dog is the first target because 'perhaps we'll get away with it if we only do the main tests'. Clearly, that's not a good general strategy. It may sometimes be necessary to reduce quality but that's a decision that you need to take both thoughtfully and cautiously.

Sometimes people think that a dog has pulled a corner of the canvas and nothing has happened – 'We got away with it' – but it's not true. A look behind the dogs will reveal claw marks in the turf where one or more has been dragged. Perhaps important tests have been skipped (Quality dog). Or perhaps staff have put in excessive unpaid overtime to meet deadlines (Resource dog). In the case of unpaid work, sooner or later the staff will get fed up with baling out badly controlled projects and look for work in better organised companies. And guess who finds it easiest to find a better job somewhere else – the best staff or the worst staff?

If you have an effective change control system, you can handle very big changes as well as the small ones. In the case of a big change you can adjust the Project Plan and Stage Plans to accommodate the additional work. In that way, the extra time and resource are allocated and the project brought back into balance – as with the control dogs in Figure 13-1.

Reducing scope creep

This section on change started with the warning that scope creep is a major project killer. In surveys of the causes of project failure, expect to see scope creep in the top five reasons, and frequently in the number one slot.

Two elements of project management help you almost eliminate scope creep. The first is a change control procedure as covered in this section. The second is clear, precise and agreed definitions of project deliverables, as explained in Chapter 5 on product planning

Chapter 14

Keeping Everyone Informed

- -

In This Chapter

▶ Identifying the underlying causes of communication problems

▶ Thinking through the communication needs in your project

▶ Establishing the most effective means of communicating

▶ Planning for communications into, within and out of the project

- -

*C*ommunications are a major source of problems in projects and are a factor frequently cited as a common cause of project failure. Such failure is unnecessary, though, because having good communications just needs some thought up front. As with so much else in this book, you won't find this chapter difficult, but it is essential.

Some projects are like a walk in the dark for the people taking part in them. They have some idea of where you are going at the outset, but then there is an information blackout. In your project, you want things to be different from those 'walk in the dark' projects. In fact, effective communication – getting the right information to and from the right people in a timely manner – is a key to successful projects.

Good communications need to be balanced. The answer to under-communication isn't over-communication – as you'll readily appreciate if your email in-box is bulging each day.

This chapter sets the scene by looking first at the underlying causes of communication problems, and then taking a quick look at the dynamics of communications. Finally, comes the practicality of planning exactly what communications you're going to need in your project and how best to carry them out.

Looking Underneath Communications Failure

Communications are a common area for problems. You don't need to think for long about day-to-day life, let alone projects, to remember misunderstandings even over simple communications. Sometimes such misunderstandings can be funny, such as the Chinese whispers party game where a spoken message is passed around a circle of people and the final version – usually hilariously – bears no resemblance whatever to the original. Funny at a party perhaps, but potentially extremely serious in a project.

Communications – a killer

If you've read other chapters in this book before coming to this one, you may react with, 'Oh no, not another project killer.' The book does indeed mention quite a few project killers, and for the very good reason that quite a few project killers exist! Communications problems are particularly significant though when you see the results of surveys into failed projects. Communications failure doesn't always take first place as the most common cause, but it's always in the top few and frequently it does occupy the number one slot.

Good communications need careful thought, and the emphasis must be on appropriate communication, carried out intelligently. Coming to the specifics of projects, what, then, are the particular underlying causes of communication problems?

Having unclear roles and responsibilities

A lot of communications problems result from unclear roles and responsibilities, where people involved in the project don't have a clear understanding of what they should be doing, and are even less clear on what other people in the project are supposed to be doing. Small wonder, then, that things drop down the gaps. Avoiding this problem is straightforward enough, and you can find help in Chapter 10 on project organisation. If project staff are absolutely clear on what they should be doing and are equally clear on the roles of others in the project, the potential for communication difficulties is immediately reduced.

Being fuzzy on products

'I've finished it. Here it is.'
'But that's not what I wanted at all! It's not even close.'
'But you said you wanted . . .'
'Yes, I did say that. But surely it was obvious that what I meant was . . .'

Great misunderstanding arises in projects over what people are to deliver. It's all too easy for people to use similar words but have different ideas, or simply to make assumptions (see the next section too) that the other person is thinking along similar lines. This is a serious communications problem because misunderstanding over deliverables, or *products*, leads to confusion, wasted work, frustration and project delay.

Turn to Chapter 5 for some serious help in avoiding product confusion, hinged on the *product-based* approach to planning. Chapter 5 includes the *Product Definition*, which sets down exactly what the product is, what quality criteria it must satisfy and how it is to be tested. Make sure that the definition, while not going into unnecessary detail that team members don't need, carries enough detail to be unambiguous. You can also involve team managers in planning – perhaps in a workshop – to discuss and even help define the deliverables.

Making assumptions

It's not the conscious assumptions that are the problem in communications, but rather the unconscious ones. You can record conscious assumptions so everyone can see them – for example: 'This plan is based on the assumption that the government grant will be authorised and the funds will be available at the start of the new financial year.' Unconscious assumptions are those that, by definition, you don't realise you're making. You just 'understand' something and don't realise that you've misunderstood. It's impossible to eliminate unconscious assumptions, but you can work, think and cross-check to reduce the number you make.

You'll do more damage to your image by pretending to have understanding when you don't than by swallowing your pride and asking the dumb questions. Don't risk making dangerous, unconscious assumptions simply because you haven't checked the facts with, perhaps, a junior team member.

Failing to feed back

When information is really important, it's helpful in a conversation to feed back to check your understanding. So many misunderstandings go undiscovered because people don't use the simple mechanism of feedback. It doesn't have to be difficult or embarrassing. You can simply say, 'That's really important. Now can I just go back through it to make sure I've got it absolutely right, and you can tell me if I've misunderstood anything?' That gives both opportunity and permission for the other person, even a very junior team member, to put you right if you have got something wrong.

Keep in mind the amusing words of author Robert McCloskey: 'I know you believe you understand what you think I said, but I'm not sure you realise that what you heard is not what I meant.'

Communicating Effectively

In your project, it helps to think through each element of the communication to understand it and then decide the best means of communication. For example, who's receiving the message? If you're communicating with technical staff, be careful not to talk down to them and explain matters when they have much more knowledge than you. On the other hand, if you're talking to trainee user staff, don't have unrealistic expectations about the amount of understanding they have of the business process you're dealing with in the project; obviously, you're going to have to spell things out and check to be quite sure they understand.

Understanding one-way and two-way communication

Some communications are one way, and others are two way:

- ✔ **One-way communication:** Going from the sender to the receiver with no opportunity for clarification or confirmation that the receiver got and correctly understood the intended message. This type of communication can be effective for presenting facts, confirming actions and sharing messages that have little chance of being misinterpreted.

One-way communications are either:

- **Push:** Proactively distributed to particular people; examples include memos, reports, letters, faxes and emails

- **Pull:** Available to people who must access the communications themselves; examples include Internet sites, knowledge repositories and bulletin boards

✔ **Two-way communication:** Going from the sender to the receiver and from the receiver back to the sender to help ensure that the intended audience received and correctly interpreted the intended message. Examples include face-to-face discussions, phone calls, in-person group meetings, interactive teleconferences and online instant messaging. Two-way communication is effective for ensuring that more complex content is correctly received and for conveying the sender's beliefs and feelings about the message.

Listening actively

The one skill that most strongly influences the quality of your communications is your ability to listen actively. Good listening skills are important to be sure that you're hearing correctly what others are saying to you, but are also important when you're checking the response of the other person to ensure that she's heard your message clearly.

Be especially careful to listen in those cases where you disagree with someone. It's fine to disagree and even to come into healthy conflict (see Chapter 12 on team dynamics). The danger of having even a healthy argument, though, is that you're so focused on getting your next point clear in your head that you fail to take on board what the other person is saying. Instead, slow down. Listen very carefully to what the other person is saying. Then don't be afraid even of leaving a short silence while you think about what the other person said before making your next point. Remember, it's no coincidence that God gave you two ears but only one mouth!

Listening is important to help you understand, but as a by-product it also has a powerful effect on those you're communicating with. Even if people disagree with you, they're much more likely to accept your authority and over-ruling of their points if they think that they have been heard. It is incredibly frustrating if you believe you have an important point but a key decision-maker hasn't taken the trouble to even listen to you. Going back to the argument in the last paragraph, you know that you would be impressed too if, when you are arguing with someone, she listens very carefully to each point that you make and stops to think about what you said before making her next contribution.

Choosing the Right Medium

When deciding how to communicate with different people in and around your project, choosing the right medium is as important as deciding what information to share. Your choice of medium helps ensure that people get the information they need when they need it.

Project communications come in two forms:

- ✔ **Planned:** Planned communications will be conducted in a form that you have to think through, even if only briefly, in advance. Examples include weekly team meetings, stakeholder briefings and monthly progress reporting.

- ✔ **Ad hoc:** Ad-hoc communications occur as people think of information they want to share. These communications occur continuously in the normal course of business. Examples include brief conversations by the water cooler and spur-of-the-moment emails you dash off during the day.

Both planned and ad-hoc communications can be either written or oral.

Beware of making an assumption that project communications all need to be written. Some communications may be carried out verbally, such as some of the reporting. The following sections look at major communications options.

Writing reports

Unlike informal oral communication, written reports enable you to present factual data efficiently, choose your words carefully to minimise misunderstandings, provide a historical record of the information you share, and share the same message with a wide audience. Written reports have benefits, they also have some drawbacks:

- ✔ They take time and effort to produce, so you need to think carefully about the frequency of regular reports.

- ✔ They don't allow your audience to ask questions to clarify the content and meaning of your message.

- ✔ With written reports alone, you can't verify that your audience received your message as you intended.

- ✔ They don't enable you to pick up nonverbal signals and they don't support interactive discussion.

- ✔ You often don't know if your report was even read!

To maximise the chances that people will read your written reports make sure that they are clear, concise and worded in a way that the readers will understand. If you were presented with a report that was full of jargon you didn't understand it, how likely are you to put it in pile to 'read later', only pressure of other work means you never quite manage to.

Preparing progress reports

Progress reports are some of the most important reports you have in the project. Progress reports operate at two levels. From Team Leaders to the Project Manager, then from the Project Manager to the steering committee (perhaps copied to others as well). Typical progress information will be:

- ✔ **Delivery:** Products produced in the stage to date.

- ✔ **Schedule:** Whether the project is on time. You might also report delivery – the Work Checklist in Chapter 13.

- ✔ **Budgets:** What staff time and money has been used so far, and how that compares with what was planned to be spent by this point. You might also show the spending against the total for the stage. For example, saying that spending has now reached 40 per cent of the stage total.

- ✔ **Performance:** How teams are performing against estimates. Are things taking more time than expected, less or is performance on track?

✔ **Risk management:** Current status of key risks and brief information on any new ones.

✔ **Other information:** Such as on significant problems currently being addressed or any other information of which the recipient(s) of the report needs to be aware.

Using a dashboard format for progress reporting

A particularly effective format for a progress report is a *dashboard* layout that resembles an instrument panel. Figure 14-1 shows some types of display on a project dashboard.

Project Alpha:
Ratio of expenditures
to budget

Project Alpha:
Schedule status of project
activities in progress

Project Alpha:
Percentage of
milestones
accomplished early
or on time to date

Figure 14-1: Typical dashboard diagrams.

When creating a dashboard for your project, be sure to:

✔ Work with the intended recipients of a report to establish the information they want to see.

✔ Always present *actual* indicator values alongside *planned* values.

✔ Keep the project dashboard report to one page or less.

Meeting up

Few words elicit the same reactions of anger and frustration that the word *meeting* can provoke. People consider meetings to be everything from the last vestige of interpersonal contact in an increasingly technical society to the biggest time waster in business today. Meetings don't have to be painful experiences, though. If you plan and manage them well, meetings can be a highly effective and concise form of communication.

Holding project meetings

Meetings you may want to hold in the project include:

- ✔ **Ad-hoc team meetings:** To discuss a problem with something being developed and get everybody's ideas for the best way of dealing with it.

- ✔ **Project progress meetings:** With the sponsor or steering committee, often every two weeks or every four weeks, to talk about progress and the outlook for the next period.

- ✔ **Regular team meetings:** Often held weekly within a team to discuss progress during the week and talk about the work in the coming week.

- ✔ **Stakeholder meetings:** To keep stakeholders up to date with what's going on in the project and help maintain interest, enthusiasm and a positive outlook. Check out Chapter 4 for more on stakeholder management.

- ✔ **Workshops:** Perhaps to sort out technical details such as a specification, but also useful for project planning, such as holding a risk workshop.

Other communication options

Following on from the earlier point that not everything has to be written down, consider the following options:

- ✔ A web site, where people can find project information.

- ✔ A short presentation with slides rather than a report.

- ✔ The telephone!

Preparing a Comms Plan

With the diversity of people who will be looking for information about your project and the array of data that you will be collecting, it's helpful and sometimes essential that you prepare a project Communications Management Plan (Comms Plan for short) to record what communications are to be made and how. As with most of project management, the Comms Plan isn't difficult.

As you come to think about project communications, it can be helpful to break them down into three areas to give more focus and structure to your thinking. Figure 14-2 shows the three areas.

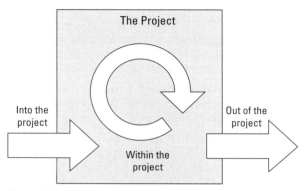

Figure 14-2: Three communication areas in a project.

Identifying communications

Within each of the three areas of communication in Figure 14-2, think through what communications are likely to take place, or which you need to set up or ask for. Then for each one, make an entry in the Comms Plan.

Identifying inbound communications

Inbound communications can be from outside the organisation, or from within the organisation but outside your project such as from other projects. Some of this information may be sent automatically, but you need to think about who'll receive it, and in other cases it won't arrive unless you specifically ask for it. You may need to include:

- ✔ Business information, such as new policies
- ✔ Financial information

✔ Inter-project information, such as new risks.

✔ Staff resource information

Circulating information within the project

You can think of internal communications within the project as being at two levels. The first is communications between the sponsor or steering committee and the Project Manager, and the second is between the Project Manger and the team leaders or team members. You can include:

✔ Change control information

✔ Direct communications to the Project Manager such as problem reporting

✔ Financial information

✔ Product development information

✔ Progress information

Sending information out of the project

Think about the following areas:

✔ Business Case information and updates

✔ Financial information

✔ Operational information, such as delivery dates

✔ Progress information

✔ Stakeholder information

Writing a Comms Plan

The Comms Plan is simply a list of the communications that will take place in the project and how they will be conducted. You can see most communications coming, but others come to light as the project progresses, so the Comms Plan must be kept up to date.

The Comms Plan lists each communication with some or all of the information in the bullet points below. For some communications, you may also need to include details of an agreed format, such as with the layout of a dashboard for a project progress report (see the section 'Using a dashboard for progress reporting', earlier in this chapter).

- ✔ **Communication name:** An easily recognisable name such as 'Team Progress Report'.

- ✔ **Security:** You may not need this heading for your project, but a surprisingly high proportion of projects do. It's not just classified data within government, but sensitive information involving clients or company plans, or privacy in the context of financial or medical records.

- ✔ **Recipient(s):** Who'll receive the communication.

- ✔ **Producer:** Who'll be responsible for the communication.

- ✔ **Content:** The information content decided or agreed for the communication.

- ✔ **Frequency:** How often the communication will be made. This may be regular such as weekly or monthly, on demand as the need arises such as with problem reporting, or fixed to a particular event such as an End of Project Report being at the end of the project.

- ✔ **Media:** How the communication will be made, such as phone call, email, website entry or business presentation.

- ✔ **Data collection:** How and when the data for the report are collected. This collection may have to be done some time in advance of the communication and involve resources beyond the person responsible for the communication, the Producer (see the earlier bullet).

Chapter 15

Closing the Project

● ●

In This Chapter

▶ Planning for a successful project termination

▶ Dealing with early closure of the project – a 'crash stop'

▶ Helping your team members move on to new work

▶ Evaluating your project's successes and failures

● ●

*O*ne characteristic that distinguishes a project from 'business as usual' work is its distinct end – the point at which all work is complete, the results are achieved (of course) and reviewed, and the project team disbanded. However, with your next assignment demanding attention, you may need to show determination in order to finish the project properly.

Not bringing your projects to full closure hurts both the organisation and the people who performed the work. When you don't assess the extent to which your project achieved the desired outcomes, you can't determine whether you conceived, planned and performed the project well. Furthermore, team members don't have the chance to experience closure, achievement and a job well done.

This chapter shows you how to close your project successfully by finishing all substantive work, performing the final administrative tasks and helping team members complete their association with your project and move on. In addition, this chapter helps you carry out a project evaluation, which is important to pick up on good and bad things that happened in this project, from which you and the organisation can take lessons to help future projects.

Most projects run their full course, but occasionally you may need to stop a project early. The early closure is a sort of 'crash stop' if something goes significantly off target or the project isn't needed anymore.

In a crash-stop situation, still look to see what can be used from the project. It's often the case that something can be saved and used, so that not all the effort is wasted. It may even be worth finishing some of the products if they're almost complete and could then be used.

Staying the Course to Completion

Projects should have a clear start and a clear finish. If you follow the product-based planning approach set out in Chapter 5, you know when the main work of the project is over, because all of the deliverables are complete. You now have some close-down work to do, which needs planning.

Thinking ahead about closure

The time to start thinking about project closure is when you're setting up the project in the first place. However, be aware that you may not be able to plan the detail until you get close to closure and can see exactly what's needed. If you wait until the end of your project to start thinking about its closure, it may be too late to gather all the necessary information and resources.

Looking at the options for closure

You have two basic options open to you for how you fit closure to project stages:

- ✔ Have a closure stage that runs after the final products have been delivered.
- ✔ Make the shutdown work part of the final delivery stage.

Amongst others, the PRIME project method strongly commends a closure stage because of the fine tuning and hand-holding work that's typical of the end of the project.

Thinking about closure from the start

If you're delivering a project to someone else, you need to be absolutely clear on how the project will be handed over at the end. There may be particular conditions for that handover, such as that project deliverables are functioning correctly, but also regarding flexibility. For example, will the customer of the project really refuse to take delivery if the 24-month project comes in 10 days overdue? It's possible that the delivery date is fixed and paramount, but in most cases you will find there is some flexibility.

An argument developed towards the end of a high-profile construction project. The construction company said that the customer should check the building, and then it could be handed over. The customer said that the building should be handed over then they would check it. The argument was finally resolved and narrowly avoided a £2 million court case that was looming to resolve the matter. Such a dispute is inexcusable in a small project, let alone a major one. The handover should be absolutely clear and agreed at the outset, and built into the plans. This is extremely easy if you use the product-planning approach covered in Chapter 5, in which the Work Flow Diagram not only shows the deliverables but also the order in which they occur. So, going back to the construction project, was 'Signed Handover Document' before 'Customer Building Check Report' or vice versa?

Dealing with a crash stop

If your project is shutting down early, perhaps because it's no longer needed because of a change in corporate policy, then you still have some planning to do for closure. The emphasis is slightly different from a planned closure, so consider the following questions for your closure plan:

- Can any of the project products be salvaged?

- Is it worth finishing any products?

- Is a review needed to see whether it could have been spotted earlier that the project was no longer viable or needed? That knowledge could save money in the future.

- Do you need to warn the organisation or individual managers that project resource will be released early?

✔ Do you need to warn finance managers that the project budget now won't be fully used?

✔ Do you need to stop supplier work prematurely and pay off remaining amounts on the contract? Of course, you'll be using that 'early shutdown' clause you had put into the contracts so you don't have to pay the full amounts!

✔ Do you need to tell the stakeholders who wanted the project that it now won't be completed? That may need particular thought and care if some stakeholders needed the project badly and the early closure has significant implications for them.

Planning Closure

As you approach the end of the project, you need to adjust your closure plans in the light of what's happening in the project, and then work them into detail so you know exactly what's involved and what time and resource will be required.

Outlining closure activities

Here are some examples of work to include in your plan:

✔ Establish what adjustments, if any, are needed to fine-tune the project deliverables, and what priority they have. Some changes may be essential and the deliverables won't be properly usable without them. Other things may be cosmetic and nice to have if they can be accommodated.

✔ Establish the amount of funding needed for adjustment, and its source. If something is a change from the original requirement (which most changes at this point will be, or the products would have failed when tested), then the customer may have to find extra budget unless the remaining change funds are sufficient.

✔ Schedule remaining work to adjust products and support user staff in their early use of them.

✔ Fix or confirm the date for the final handover and the close of the project.

✔ Check any business benefits that are immediately visible at the end of the project.

✔ Check the plans for measuring and reporting benefits that won't be visible until after the project has shut down.

✔ Identify any elements of project control that will need to be passed forward into the working life of products. This includes version control systems, risk management and maintenance requirements.

✔ Terminate contracts for project work and pass on to the business area any contracts for ongoing supplies and support. This includes authorising any final payments..

✔ Ensure that all support documentation is in place for ongoing maintenance and operations.

✔ Ensure that any necessary licences, permits or other authorities are in place, ready for handover.

✔ Plan the release of project staff, because support requirements will wind down during closure, liaising as needed with their line managers, and then release staff in line with the plan.

✔ List any organisational actions that will be needed or which are recommended after the project. This might include picking up on good ideas that the project didn't have time to implement, or adjusting project management standards following experience in this project.

Although not necessarily appearing on the official list of project closure work, some sort of project celebration is appropriate for a successful project. It's not only right to thank staff for their part in the success of the project, but it's a great boost to see and celebrate the result of all the effort.

Providing a Good Transition

Team members can get very concerned when it's first suggested that they move over to work on your project. How team members get back into the mainstream after the project, or onto a new project is extremely important. In some organisations, being assigned to a project is seen as a career death sentence. You not only need to make sure that arrangements are in hand for the return of staff, but that these arrangements are carried through.

Even if bad things don't happen to team members after a project, they're likely to worry that they will. The transition back to ordinary work needs to be planned and explained.

Reviewing the Project

Lay the groundwork for repeating on future projects what worked well on this one (and avoiding what didn't) by conducting a project evaluation or review.

A *project evaluation* is an assessment of project results, activities and processes. It contributes to noting lessons learned (both good things and bad things) that will help improve project management on future projects.

Avoid the term *project post-mortem* because it conjures up the image of an autopsy to determine the cause of death! The term alone gives people a very negative outlook and suggests that the evaluation is looking only for problems and culprits. The project review is as much, or even more, about what went well as what went badly.

Beginning with the end in mind

The second habit in Stephen Covey's book *The 7 Habits of Highly Effective People* is 'Begin with the end in mind'. That's great advice when it comes to project review. You can't review properly unless you have something to review against. Right at the beginning of the project, you need to think what you'll review against. Just think about what you want to check at the end of the project and then put in place the things that will enable you to carry out that check, such as:

- ✔ Benefits
- ✔ Finance targets
- ✔ Meeting deadlines – perhaps key deliveries that need to be made during the project as well as at the end
- ✔ Objectives – what the project is to achieve
- ✔ Productivity levels
- ✔ Quality
- ✔ Risk mitigation

You can conduct a review by going around and talking to people or by a meeting that you can hold in person, or by video or in a telephone conference. As always, face to face is better, so only resort to other means when you really must. A good review, whether by interview or meeting, requires that you address the right topics and that people share their project thoughts and experiences openly and honestly.

As you plan your consultation with others, consider asking about the following issues:

- ✔ Could anything have been done better, faster or more cheaply?

- ✔ If you did the project again, what would you like to be done differently in the light of this project experience?

- ✔ If you did the project again, what would you like to see done the same way next time because it worked so well?

- ✔ Was anything unnecessary and, if so, was that just because of the way things turned out or because, on reflection, the activity was over the top from the outset?

- ✔ With any mistakes or misunderstandings, could someone have seen them coming and prevented them, or were they just the sort of things that you can never completely eliminate?

- ✔ Could anything have made your work easier, such as more support or better equipment?

- ✔ With regard to problems during the project:

  - • Could you have anticipated and planned for them? If so, how?

  - • Did you handle them effectively and efficiently when they arose?

- ✔ Did you use the organisation's project management systems and procedures effectively?

- ✔ Were any of the organisation's project management systems ineffective or inappropriate? If so, should this type of project be exempted from such procedures, or should the procedures be changed for all projects?

Recording project information

For many of the review areas, having established at the outset that you'll review them, you then need to set up mechanisms to record the data so that you can review it at the end. Finance is an obvious one, and you'll undoubtedly be recording spending information anyway, but what about quality and what about team performance? Just how many products did fail test and need rework? Did the teams deliver products within the expected number of staff hours, or was the number of hours significantly less or more?

As we explain in the introduction to this chapter, project review brings to light important information, and missing it out damages the organisation. Project review shouldn't normally be a huge amount of work, but the information that flows out of it can be hugely valuable for future projects.

Learning lessons

There's a clear and obvious link between project review and learning lessons to be passed on to future projects, but the two aren't the same thing. Some aspects of review, such as whether the project met its objectives, are usually for this project alone. Similarly, lessons learned may be identified and passed on throughout the life of the project, particularly if it is a long one, not just left to the end.

Identifying the cause of problems in order to avoid them on future projects is very important, but the main thrust of lessons learned is to see what worked really well and pass on that experience so other projects can benefit.

Having learned lessons, you must then pass them on and not just leave them to get dusty along with the other project records in some forgotten corner of a network drive. Future Project Managers must be able to get at the lessons easily.

Measuring benefits

If benefits are visible at the end of the project, which some may be, no sponsor is going to wait six months for some post-projec benefits review if there's already some indication as to whether the project has been a success.

Many benefits won't be clear for some time. For example, if the project has put some new business process in place and at the end of the project the business staff start to use it, it's no good looking at time savings immediately. Staff will still be going slowly as they learn the new approach. The best time to measure the time saving of the new procedure will probably be in four or six weeks' time when things have settled down and staff are up to a normal speed of working.

Measuring benefits now

While the project is still running, there are either one or two end points where you may want to measure and report benefits. Whether there are one or two points depends on whether you have a closure stage or if closure is just at the end of the final delivery stage.

When final products are delivered, some benefits may be seen immediately, such as that maintenance time drops as soon as the new machines are commissioned and the old ones are taken out of service, or that customer complaints are dramatically reduced the moment the new delivery procedures start up. You can measure and report such benefits at the end of the final delivery stage, which in some approaches may mark the end of the project.

If you have a closure stage, though, it may well be that the six-week measures can be taken within the life of the project, before final closure, and reported.

Measuring benefits later

If benefits will come on stream after the end of the project, either because you don't have a closure stage or because the benefits will take a longer time to become clear, then it's not within the remit of the project to measure and report on them. However, you should make arrangements for such measures and reporting back to corporate management on the eventual level of benefit from the project.

It's vital that the organisation does review project benefits systematically or else poor management decisions may be made in the future.

Nick Graham was talking to staff from a local authority in Scotland about their current project, its justification and its projected benefits. The staff told him that the project was justified because it would make a 5 per cent saving. When he asked how that had been calculated, the staff told him that it hadn't been, but it would surely save at least 5 per cent. When he asked if they would measure at the end of the project to check the saving, he was told that they never did, because the pressure to do other projects was so great they just moved straight on to the next one. Nick said, 'Don't tell me, you justify the next project on a 5 per cent saving as well!' He intended it as a light-hearted remark, but to his astonishment the staff replied seriously, 'Yes, that's right.'

Passing Work On

The final part of the closure work is to consider what work needs to be passed on to organisational managers such as operations staff. The nature of this post-project work varies depending on the nature of the organisation and the project, but here are a few areas to think about:

✓ Considering changes to organisational standards and procedures such as project procedures and risk handling

✓ Making sure that if suppliers delivered sub-standard items that were temporarily usable, but not correct, that the supplier replaces those items

✓ Incorporating maintenance work

✓ Measuring and reporting benefits that will come on stream after the end of the project

✓ Picking up on good ideas developed during the project but which the project didn't have time or money to do

✓ Monitoring risk-related work that's ongoing, such as use of dangerous machinery

✓ Enforcing version control

In each case, discuss the work with the person who'll be taking it on to be sure that he's the right person and that he has the capacity to do the job. If there's a problem, discuss it with your sponsor or steering committee, but make sure that it's resolved so that the item isn't left unmanaged.

Chapter 16

Using Technology to Up Your Game

• •

• •

A major part of project management is information – getting it, creating it, storing it, analysing it and sharing it. But the key to successful project management is using this information to see what's going on in the project and exercise control, and to guide and encourage people's performance.

Technology is providing ever easier and more affordable ways to handle information and also to help with the work involved in areas such as project planning. For example, computer software allows you to enter, store and analyse information and then present the results in professional formats. Email allows written communication with people in remote locations at all hours of the day (and night!), and video conferencing allows you to talk to them too. Computer scheduling tools allow you to draw up activity networks and Gantt Charts (see Chapter 6) much more quickly and easily, but then also help you to make changes easily and rapidly and so keep the plans up to date.

This chapter shows how you can use technology in jobs that benefit from it. It starts with a warning on what technology can't do, such as making key project decisons for you.

Using Software Effectively

Software for special analyses, project planning and reporting now looks so good that you may be tempted to believe it's all you need to ensure project success. However, even though the software works effectively and efficiently, it *can't*:

✔ **Ensure that information is appropriately defined, timely and accurate.** In most instances, people record information to support project planning and control, and then they enter the information into a computer. You can set up the software to check for correctness of format or internal consistency, but the software can't ensure the quality and integrity of the data.

Suppose you use a computer program to maintain records of work hours that team members charge to your project. You can get time-recording software to reject hours that are inadvertently charged with an invalid project code. However, you can't set the package to recognise hours charged to the wrong project with a valid code.

✔ **Analyse all information or make project decisions.** Software can help you objectively determine the results of several possible courses of action. However, software can't effectively take into account all the objective and subjective considerations that you must weigh up before making a final decision.

✔ **Create and sustain dynamic interpersonal relationships.** Despite people's fascination with Facebook, email, texts and other types of social networking, computers can't ensure trusting relationships between people working together on a team. Technology can even make relationships more difficult to develop. Developments such as video communications through Skype and similar services help because they give some ability to see facial expressions and body language, but it's still nowhere near as good as face-to-face communication, and the limited duration of each communication isn't the same as working alongside a colleague in a team room.

So how *can* computer facilities help you during the life of a project? This section looks at what functionality is available and how technology can help you manage your project.

Seeing what software you need

You'll find computer software helpful in three core areas:

✓ **Office software:** This is the standard package of a word processor, spreadsheet, presentation software and, possibly, database and contacts (address book) functionality. The presentation software gives some graphics capability, and perhaps enough for your needs, but you may choose a different package for graphics.

✓ **Project management software:** Well, so-called project management software anyway. The *so called* is because the packages are mostly scheduling software to do activity networks, Gantt Charts and resource scheduling. There is much more to project management than that, as you can discover by flicking through this book.

✓ **Communication software:** This includes email, but also things like RSS feeds (to notify changed information on a website), tweeting and, perhaps more importantly, Skype and its equivalents for video calls.

An area where software may be necessary, not merely a benefit, is if you're maintaining a website for your project and need web management facilities. Then again you may need software support for things like version control, MindMap diagrams and time management. This chapter focuses primarily on the core areas that cover the bulk of the project management work you'll encounter.

Knowing where to use software

It's pretty obvious where you use some of the software. If you want to do an activity network, you'll naturally be drawn to a project management package. However, some uses aren't so obvious, so this section points out where you might use software applications and where you might use them in more unusual circumstances if you need to or even have to.

Office software

Office software is important for things like reporting, but remember that a report may be in the form of a presentation to a steering committee or project board, where the presentation element of the software will be more than useful. The most common package is Microsoft Office, but there are others.

Here's some core software you'll need:

- ✔ **Database:** Useful for things like a Risk Register and a Project Log, if you want something with more power than a spreadsheet.

- ✔ **Presentation graphics:** Useful for reporting and passing on information in the form of a presentation, but the facilities in these packages are powerful for general graphics work too and are great for things like the product-planning diagrams.

- ✔ **Spreadsheet:** Budget information, 'what if' calculations and also reporting if you use a 'dashboard' format for progress reports (see Chapter 15). Interestingly, spreadsheets are widely used for resource planning in larger projects, where many Project Managers find that the project management software just doesn't give them the flexibility and detail they need. You might also hold register overviews on a spreadsheet, such as a summary of information from the Risk Register. You can even produce an activity network on a spreadsheet, but it's hard work both in creating the network and then keeping it up to date, and project management (scheduling) software is considerably better. If you're thinking that you can't afford project management software, have a look at the section 'Getting Good Stuff for Free', later in this chapter.

- ✔ **Word processor:** For written communications, including reporting, and document preparation such as the Project Charter. You might also produce a project news sheet if you need to keep stakeholders informed of developments and you don't need the sophistication of desktop publishing software.

Project management software

This title is a misnomer because the package doesn't help with all of project management or anything approaching it. Really, the tools are scheduling tools and cover activity networks, Gantt Charts and resource planning including resource levelling. The best known is Microsoft Project, but there are many others.

Project-scheduling software is generally excellent in what it does, but it can prove very frustrating as well because of the limitations it can impose. As you get used to the software, you quickly learn the tricks to make it display what you want, even if that means telling 'lies' to the software to get the effect you need. On the other hand, though, who'd want to recalculate a hand-drawn, 100-task, two-year duration activity network because a duration changed in Week 1?

Some packages are available that fit with project methods, but be careful to check what they do, what they don't do and the nature of their support. These tools, for example, generally don't include scheduling functionality but require you to use something like Microsoft Project alongside them. Some also start at the wrong end. They provide a huge amount of documentation and the boast that the software will help you control it all. A better start is to minimise the documentation and limit it to what you really need, not get help controlling some vast and unnecessary project bureaucracy.

A typical project management package allows you to:

✔ Create a hierarchical list of activities and their components.

✔ Define and store key information about your project, activities and resources.

✔ Define activity interdependencies (see Chapter 6 for more information on activity interdependencies).

✔ Develop schedules by considering activity durations, activity interdependencies, and resource requirements and availability.

✔ Display your plan for performing project activities in a network diagram (see Chapter 6).

✔ Display a schedule in Gantt Chart and table formats (see Chapter 6).

✔ Assign people to work on project activities for specific levels of effort at certain times.

✔ Schedule other resources for project activities at specified times.

✔ Determine your overall project budget (see Chapter 7 for help on project budgets).

✔ Determine the effect of changes on the project's schedule and resources.

✔ Monitor activity start and end dates and milestone dates.

✔ Monitor person-hours and resource costs.

✔ Present planning and tracking information in a wide array of graphs and tables.

Project management packages offer further benefits including:

✔ **The package's functions are linked.** For example, if you enter staff availability in the form of personal calendars, the program uses them when developing the schedule and won't allow an activity for a team member to run in a week when she'll be on holiday.

✔ **Packages typically have a variety of predesigned report templates.** Having predesigned report templates allows you to use formats that are proven to be effective. It also saves you time and money when preparing and distributing your reports.

Before you rush out and buy any project management software, plan how to maximise its capabilities and avoid associated pitfalls. Do the following to help you select and install your software:

✔ Be sure you have a firm grasp of project planning and control approaches and techniques before you consider any software.

✔ See what software other groups in your organisation are using or have used; find out what they like, what they don't like and why.

✔ If possible, ask someone who already has a copy of the software whether you can spend a few minutes exploring its operation.

✔ After the package is on your computer, load a simple project or a small part of a larger project to practise with (that is, enter the activities, durations, interdependencies, resources and so on).

✔ Use only a few of the program's capabilities at first (determine the effect of small changes on your schedule, print out some simple reports, and so on); use more capabilities as you get more comfortable with the software and feel the need for the facilities.

> ✔ Consider attending a formal training course after you've become comfortable accessing the software's different capabilities.

After you've undertaken these steps, you can effectively use software to support your project planning and control activities. On an ongoing basis, ensure that you obtain all updates and changes to the software, and consider purchasing software upgrades that introduce significant new capabilities.

Communications management software

Communications problems are a primary cause of project failure, so the whole area of communications in your project justifies some very careful thought; Chapter 14 goes into the detail. Technology can help with communication but it can also hinder it, so you need to keep your brain in gear when considering communication.

Communications technology is particularly good when it adds something that can't easily be done otherwise, and this section covers five examples.

Tweeting

A relatively new technology is tweeting using the Twitter social networking service. Having first been associated with teenagers filling their many spare hours with idle chatter, its potential was quickly spotted by other and perhaps more serious users. Organisations such as political parties in the UK have been quick to see the value of keeping people in touch, but so have businesses to keep customers informed of the latest services and offers and to keep their names regularly in front of the customers.

In the context of a project, tweeting may be worth considering to keep information flowing to large teams who are spread out geographically, but also as a mechanism for keeping key stakeholders in touch with developments in a fast-moving project environment.

Emailing

Email is powerful, and would be more powerful still if it wasn't so widely misused. Disciplined use of email makes for rapid and powerful communication, as you will be well aware.

Video conferencing

Where you need a meeting, nothing beats face-to-face, but where that's difficult or expensive, then video calls over the phone are great substitutes. You get better communication when you can see people and gauge their reactions in a discussion. With international projects in particular, the video conference is a powerful and economic addition to your communication options.

Working collaboratively with software

Major players such as Microsoft increasingly allow for online collaborative working with their software. An example is with a shared 'whiteboard' where people can join in remotely to add to diagrams and comment, but collaborative environments often offer shared file storage as well.

Collaborative working like this comes second place to working around a whiteboard face to face. However, if getting everyone together isn't possible or is prohibitively expensive, then such electronic collaboration is much better than phone calls during which participants can't see diagrams and certainly can't directly draw onto the diagrams. Email is worse, with the inbuilt time delay. Using online collaborative environments also retains the 'shared experience' dynamic where ideas spark backwards and forwards more easily and where participants get more engaged than they would with some form of written response.

Setting up a website

A useful technology in bigger projects is . . . the web. A website dedicated to the project can be extraordinarily effective both in making information available and keeping people in touch with the project.

Part of the advantage of setting up a website relates to the problem of email distribution lists. If you have a website for your project, then you can email your fellow Project Managers, once, to say that you have a site and if they want to know anything about your project then to go and look on the site. They'll be extremely grateful that you haven't merely added them to yet another email group to pump megabytes of text into their inboxes 'in case they want to know'. Hopefully, they'll be so impressed and appreciative that they'll follow suit and set up websites for their projects and stop sending you trayfuls of email 'in case you want to know'. You'll find more in Chapter 14 about the implications of using this technology to circulate project information.

A second way that a website can be really useful is to keep people in touch with, and interested in, your project. If you have a public interface or customers who are very interested in how things are going, then a website could be the answer.

In terms of project information held on the site, adding an RSS feed makes it even more useful. With RSS, as you're probably aware from your own use of the web, people who are subscribed get notified automatically when something has changed, and don't need to keep checking the site themselves.

Every Cloud Has a Silver Lining

Cloud computing is now with us, and its use is expanding very rapidly. A *cloud* is where you have data and even software stored centrally by an Internet service and you access that data over the Internet. Cloud computing is exciting for projects because it makes access to data so much easier (working at home as well as in the office) and because it brings with it functionality like computer synchronisation.

If you store your project data in a cloud, then everyone to whom you give the necessary authority can access it over the Internet, wherever they are in the world and at any time of the day or night. If you update a file and upload it, then immediately everyone has access to that new version.

Many cloud services incorporate synchronisation of data. Each computer has a copy of the cloud on its local disk and from time to time will check that the local copy is an exact copy of the folders and files on the cloud. If the local computer has a more recent file (because the user has updated or created something) it will be sent up to the cloud, and if the cloud has a more recent copy or something new, it will be downloaded to that local computer.

The speed at which computers are synchronised varies with the service you are using. Some only synchronise at intervals, so there can be a gap before the new file goes up to the cloud and another gap before other computers check the cloud and download any changes. Other services are almost instantaneous, such as Dropbox and will push data down where it has changed; it doesn't work by timed checks.

This section of Project Management For Dummies is hard to write because even before the book gets published, things will inevitably have changed. However, in an attempt to be helpful, here are three simple guidelines on cloud computing:

✔ **Back up:** Commercial cloud storage is reliable, but don't rely on it. Don't keep a backup copy of your files either; keep several (!) and in different places too. Just two sorts of computer hard disk exist: those that are going to fail and those that have already failed.

✔ **Be careful with synchronisation:** Synchronisation is great, but it has a drawback. If some junior team member deletes a file on her local copy of the cloud, that deletion instruction will get transmitted up to the cloud and then onto everyone else's computers, and the file will be wiped out everywhere. The more sophisticated suppliers of cloud services have an archive from which you can retrieve deleted stuff as much as six months afterwards. That archive service is valuable, provided you realise in time that something has been accidentally deleted.

✔ **Watch security:** Cloud storage is not 100 per cent secure even if you have got good access controls. That lack of security can simply be because a rookie team member has written her complicated 'secure' password on a sticky note and stuck it on the wall above her desk. But even if the access and the cloud storage itself is safe, the transmission of data to and from that storage generally isn't. Storing information such as project plans is probably going to be fine. But you probably shouldn't put important commercial information on your company's finances that's embedded in the project Business Case on cloud storage.

Getting Good Stuff for Free

No, it's true, you can. Powerful, reliable and highly functional services and software are available for free on both PC and

Mac platforms. Software includes *freeware*, but more significantly you can download *open source* software, which is the fruit of collaboration on a huge scale worldwide.

A search on the Internet can help you find such software and services. New stuff is emerging all the time, but this section gives you a starting place and also provides a few hints on what to look out for:

- **Activity planning:** Lots of free tools are highly functional for activity networks, Gantt Charts and resource planning (see Chapter 6). They're the equivalent of Microsoft Project. You find them for both PC and Mac platforms, and a sophisticated example for the PC is Open Workbench.

- **Cloud storage:** Internet service providers often give some online cloud storage (see the previous section) for free. Other commercial services are paid for but can be free in two respects. First, you can sometimes get a fairly generous trial period for free, and that period may actually be enough for your project. Apple's MobileMe service currently offers six months use for free. Second, some services like Dropbox give a basic amount of storage for free, but you then pay if you want more. That last option might not sound so good until you see just how generous the free allowance is; it's quite substantial when you are storing things like documents rather than large libraries of music and photographs. Having said that, even if you do want more space, the extra storage is usually reasonably priced and available in increments.

- **Mind Mapping:** Many free packages are impressively functional. These are great if you like Mind Maps and want to use them for product planning and risk analysis.

- **Office packages:** Many cheap office packages offer word processor, spreadsheet and graphics programs, but you also have the choice of some free ones. The most widely recognised is Open Office, which is available on both PC and Mac platforms. Open Office has the advantage that it is very powerful and it reads in and out of Microsoft Office formats.

Watching out for file formats

When looking at the free software, check out the file formats
and the import and export features. You need to ensure that
you can communicate with other people. It's no good working
late into the night at home on an update to your project plan
if you can't then load the file into the software at the office.

Obeying security restrictions

In all cases when you're shifting data about, do make sure you
take on board any security restrictions in your organisation.
It takes the shine off delivering a really successful project if
you then get fired for security violations. In this context, security includes virus-checking procedures. Don't think either
that viruses don't matter if you're in the happy world of Macs
because, of course, nasty things can find their way into macro-
enabled documents as well as programs and operating systems.

Saving Time with Software

Using computers can make life much easier for the Project
Manager. It can also make for great time savings:

- **Easy retrieval:** For other project staff, not just the
  Project Manager, to get at documents quickly, but also
  to be able to retrieve an older version. Which, in passing,
  means that you should routinely save the different ver-
  sions of project documents.

- **Fast transmission:** A report sent as an email attachment
  rather than through the mail – internal mail, national or
  international.

- **Fast update:** Such as putting new estimates based on
  recent information into an activity network then recalcu-
  lating the critical path (see Chapter 6) before printing off
  a new version of the plan.

- **Re-use:** Storing project documentation such as plans that
  might be adapted for future similar projects, so saving
  time and helping ensure completeness.

- **Template documents**: A stock of basic templates for
  things like budgets and reports that save having to start
  from scratch for each project.

Part V
The Part of Tens

'And what happens to the project leader
if the project goes wrong?'

In this part . . .

*H*aving hundreds of pages of detailed information to guide you through your project's ups and downs is nice. However, for some areas it's good to have a few handy tips in a concise form.

Just like every *For Dummies* book, this part gives you tidbits of interesting information that you can access as needed. There are ten tips for how to plan a project and ten for writing a convincing Business Case.

Chapter 17

Ten Questions to Ask Yourself for Project Planning

- -

In This Chapter

▶ Clarifying your project's objective

▶ Describing deliverables, schedules and resources

▶ Addressing the uncertainties

- -

*W*hen you begin a project, enthusiasm or organisational deadlines, or both, can make you want to jump in and start working on the detail immediately. However, you know you have the greatest chance of a successful outcome, including delivering the right thing, if you plan out your project before you start the actual work. Answer the ten questions in this chapter to be sure you've completely identified all the work your project will require.

What Are the Objectives?

A common cause of project problems to the point of failure is unclear objectives. Check the following:

✔ Exactly what is the project being asked to deliver?

✔ What is the primary purpose of the project? Perhaps to speed up delivery to customers, comply with legal requirements, save money, or more than one..

✔ Who'll benefit from the project?

✔ What would happen if the project wasn't run?

Who Do You Need to Involve?

Knowing early on who you need to involve allows you to plan for their participation. Think about:

- **Budget holders:** People who hold the purse strings.
- **Providers:** Those providing any staff resource that you need. For example, do you need IT staff input, which may be difficult if the IT department is mostly committed for the next two years!
- **Stakeholders:** People who have an interest in your project's results. You may need to resolve conflicting objectives.
- **Supporters:** People who can help your project succeed.

What Will You Produce?

Be clear on what the project is delivering in total, then in more detail as you get into project planning. Make sure that the key players agree the key deliverables or products. You may even produce a few Product Definitions when sketching out the project, because often people get a much clearer view of what the project is about when they understand what it will deliver.

- Think through what products you'll need to generate.
- Define those products carefully, involving others where necessary.
- Determine the sequence in which products need to be produced and the dependencies between them.

Are There Any Constraints?

Identify all information, processes and guidelines that may restrict your project activities and your performance. When you know your constraints, you can plan effectively to work within them if, for example, they are technical or time constraints, and to minimise their effects on your project if they relate to something like financial or staffing availability.

Identify whether any constraints can be challenged. For example, with a technical constraint, you may be able to challenge an instruction to use a certain type of machine if a new machine becomes available that's better and cheaper.

What Are the Assumptions?

As soon as you begin thinking about your project, document all conscious assumptions you make about it, and think very hard so you can minimise the unconscious ones.

What Work Has to Be Done?

Identify all the activities required to produce your project's products so that you can assign responsibilities for them, develop schedules, estimate resource needs, give specific tasks to team members and monitor your project's performance. For each activity, specify the following:

- ✔ **The work to be done:** The processes and steps that each activity entails

- ✔ **Inputs:** All people, facilities, equipment, supplies, raw materials, funds and information necessary to perform each activity

- ✔ **Durations:** The number of work periods required to perform each activity

When Will Each Activity Happen?

Develop a detailed schedule:

- ✔ **Duration:** The number of work periods required to perform each individual activity

- ✔ **External dependencies:** Such as on other projects

- ✔ **Interdependencies:** What you must finish before you can begin your activity

- ✔ **Resource availability:** When you need particular resources and when they're available (see the next section as well)

Who Will Do the Project Work?

Knowing who will perform each task and how much effort they'll have to devote allows you to plan for their availability and more accurately estimate the overall project budget. Think about:

- The skills and knowledge needed to build each product
- The actual people needed on each activity and any specific roles they may have, such as team leaders and specialists
- The amount of time needed by each person
- The exact time when people will do their work if they will work less than full time on an activity

Consult with the people who'll perform the project tasks to develop this information. See Chapter 7 for help with estimating staffing requirements.

Do You Need Other Resources?

Identify all equipment, facilities, services, supplies and funds that you need to perform your project work. Specify how much of each resource you need and when.

What Can Go Wrong?

Don't be taken off guard. Identify risks and develop sensible plans to minimise their negative effects. See Chapter 10 for information on how to address project risks, and remember that some risk actions may be very simple, quick and cheap, but can work to prevent your project coming under unnecessary pressure.

Lisa Faulkner, winner of the TV cookery award *Celebrity MasterChef 2010*, said, just before the final, 'My food has to be fault-free today. It has to look good and taste good. And there are little things that could go wrong but I've got backup plans so that if they do go wrong I can turn them around into things that have gone right.' Good project advice!

Chapter 18

Ten Tips for Writing a Convincing Business Case

In This Chapter

▶ Being prudent and not 'over-egging' the Business Case

▶ Being clear on what are benefits and what are technical features

▶ Seeing things from a business, rather than a project, viewpoint

A project needs to be justified, not just done for the sake of it. You often need to set down that justification in the form of a Business Case, which, as the name suggests, explains the case for the project from a business perspective. It's easy to go off track in a Business Case so that managers in the organisation who have the authority to approve the project simply aren't convinced and so don't give the go-ahead. This chapter sets out ten tips to help you get the Business Case right first time.

Starting with a Bang

Your project will normally have a number of benefits, and it can really help to start with the best one – start with a bang. That grabs the attention and gets people on side quickly. Don't exaggerate this benefit, but do let it have its full impact in the way that you write it. For example: 'This project will save £1 million in reduced wastage in the first three years of operation.' Notice that the £1 million figure is rather more impressive than saying £333,000 a year. If you think that sounds a bit like a sales pitch, you're right. You need to 'sell' the project idea in order to get the green light.

On the other hand, this is a business document, so although you should sell the idea, the Business Case should contain solid, evidenced business information and not be frothy sales talk.

If you're using a format in which the benefits aren't the first thing in the Business Case but something like a summary or a management overview is, use the opening of that to make the bang with the biggest benefit.

Spelling Out the Benefits Clearly

Spell out the benefits of the project in clear terms that those reading the document can relate to. You can find it all too easy to be convinced of the project yourself within the project perspective, where it all makes perfect sense, but fail to see things as people outside the project see them.

If your project is of any size beyond small, then with benefits you need to be particularly aware of the senior management perspective and, specifically, the financial management perspective. To a finance director and a managing director, a direct saving is very different to a quantifiable benefit and again to a non-quantifiable benefit. Direct savings make directors sit up quickly and take notice, so be sure to point these out. If you aren't sure of the difference between quantifiable and non-quantifiable benefits, have a look at Chapter 3 for an explanation.

Identifying Non-quantifiables

You should explain non-quantifiable benefits especially carefully and back up claims of these benefits and your estimates of their significance. Non-quantifiables can be extremely important in business terms, but as hinted in the previous section, senior managers tend to focus on the money; often they are less interested in the non-quantifiables. When non-quantifiables are important, explain why.

Being Prudent

Don't overstate or exaggerate benefits. Remember the financial principle of being prudent and erring on the safe side. If you make huge claims for the project that it can't deliver, it (and you) will be seen as a failure when those benefits don't materialise. If you slightly understate the benefits, you have a margin for error, but also if you slightly exceed them the project (and you) will be seen as a success.

Once again, you need to strike a balance with this. If you massively understate the benefits, then when your project delivers considerably more you'll be seen in a bad light for not having set down an accurate Business Case and not understanding the nature and impact of your project.

Using Three-point Estimating

Sometimes you just can't be sure of the benefits levels, or you're in difficulty because some enthusiastic manager has already told everyone that the project won't cost much, will take almost no time at all, and will deliver mind-boggling benefits. To deal with either scenario, you can set down three projections of each benefit: best case, worst case and then the most likely case.

Checking Benefits Aren't Features

If you have a technical interest in the project (you're a 'techie') you may be rather too focused on the technical aspects rather than the business advantages. Having a 2-nanosecond transmission time through the outer core of the flange assembly may be the latest groundbreaking technology, but it's a technical feature not a business benefit. In all cases, think 'how does this benefit the business?'

It could well be that the technology represents substantial business benefit, but you must then spell that benefit out. If the faster speed means that production costs will be reduced, then that becomes a business benefit and one which can be quantified and, later, measured and proved.

Avoiding Benefits Contamination

Inspirandum coined the phrase *benefits contamination* to describe projects that claim benefits that are really due to something else outside the project.

Financial managers usually have a keen eye for benefits, and if they spot such contamination then it undermines your credibility and the credibility of the whole Business Case. Also, if you're claiming benefits that won't actually be delivered by the project, it could lead to the project being approved when actually that's not the right decision.

Making Sure You Can Deliver

When setting down the benefits, make quite sure that they can be delivered. If you're showing savings from the sale of a building, are you absolutely sure that someone wants to buy it? If not, state your assumption that the building will be sold within a reasonable time. In turn, it would be helpful to back up the point with some stats on the average time taken to sell a building of that type in that locality at the moment.

Backing Up Your Claims

Where you're claiming business benefits, you should back those claims up with evidence. However, if the evidence already exists, then you can simply reference it. For example:

> *As stated by Go-4-It Consultants in their report presented to directors last June, the new packaging options that will be delivered by this project are likely to boost sales by 5 per cent, which represents an annual profit increase of £XXX.*

Using Appendices

Don't hesitate to use appendices in the Business Case; you don't need to shove everything into the main body of the document. You may want to use appendices for two reasons:

- ✔ **Where you have an organisational standard:** In that case, put the extra project-only information in appendices and don't submit them to the finance committee.

- ✔ **Keeping the Business Case simple**: If the Business Case is to be seen by senior managers in particular, it helps enormously to keep it short and simple. Detailed calcualtions can go into an appendix that readers can dip into if they want to.

Index

• *D* •

FOR DUMMIES®

Making Everything Easier! ™

UK editions

BUSINESS

Marketing Kit
FOR DUMMIES

978-0-470-74490-1

Business Plans Kit
FOR DUMMIES

978-0-470-74381-2

PRINCE2
FOR DUMMIES

978-0-470-71025-8

REFERENCE

British Politics
FOR DUMMIES

978-0-470-68637-9

DIY
FOR DUMMIES

978-0-470-97450-6

Researching Your
Family History Online
FOR DUMMIES

978-0-470-74535-9

HOBBIES

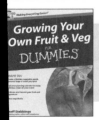

Growing Your
Own Fruit & Veg
FOR DUMMIES

978-0-470-69960-7

Allotment Gardening
FOR DUMMIES

978-0-470-68641-6

Electronics
FOR DUMMIES

978-0-470-68178-7

Anger Management
For Dummies
978-0-470-68216-6

Asperger's Syndrome
For Dummies
978-0-470-66087-4

Boosting Self-Esteem
For Dummies
978-0-470-74193-1

British Sign Language
For Dummies
978-0-470-69477-0

Cricket For Dummies
978-0-470-03454-5

Diabetes For Dummies,
3rd Edition
978-0-470-97711-8

Emotional Healing
For Dummies
978-0-470-74764-3

English Grammar
For Dummies
978-0-470-05752-0

Flirting For Dummies
978-0-470-74259-4

Football For Dummies
978-0-470-68837-3

Healthy Mind & Body All-in-One
For Dummies
978-0-470-74830-5

IBS For Dummies
978-0-470-51737-6

Improving Your Relationship
For Dummies
978-0-470-68472-6

Nutrition For Dummies,
2nd Edition
978-0-470-97276-2

FOR DUMMIES®

The easy way to get more done and have more fun

FOR

DUMMIES®

Helping you expand your horizons and achieve your potential

COMPUTER BASICS

978-0-470-57829-2

978-0-470-46542-4

978-0-470-49743-2

DIGITAL PHOTOGRAPHY

978-0-470-25074-7

978-0-470-46606-3

978-0-470-59591-6

MICROSOFT OFFICE 2010

978-0-470-48998-7

978-0-470-58302-9

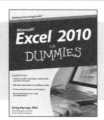

978-0-470-48953-6

Access 2010 For Dummies
978-0-470-49747-0

Android Application Development
For Dummies
978-0-470-77018-4

AutoCAD 2011 For Dummies
978-0-470-59539-8

C++ For Dummies, 6th Edition
978-0-470-31726-6

Computers For Seniors For Dummies
2nd Edition
978-0-470-53483-0

Dreamweaver CS5 For Dummies
978-0-470-61076-3

Green IT For Dummies
978-0-470-38688-0

iPad All-in-One For Dummies
978-0-470-92867-7

Macs For Dummies, 11th Edition
978-0-470-87868-2

Mac OS X Snow Leopard For Dummies
978-0-470-43543-4

Photoshop CS5 For Dummies
978-0-470-61078-7

Photoshop Elements 9 For Dummies
978-0-470-87872-9

Search Engine Optimization
For Dummies, 4th Edition
978-0-470-88104-0

The Internet For Dummies,
12th Edition
978-0-470-56095-2

Visual Studio 2010 All-In-One
For Dummies
978-0-470-53943-9

Web Analytics For Dummies
978-0-470-09824-0

Word 2010 For Dummies
978-0-470-48772-3